The GROUND
of LOVE
and TRUTH

The GROUND
of LOVE
and TRUTH

Reflections on

THOMAS MERTON'S
relationship with the woman
known as "M"

SUZANNE ZUERCHER, O.S.B.

in extenso

THE GROUND OF LOVE AND TRUTH
Reflections on Thomas Merton's Relationship
with the Woman Known as "M"
by Suzanne Zuercher, O.S.B.

Edited by Gregory F. Augustine Pierce
Cover design, interior design, and typesetting by Patricia A. Lynch

Numerous excerpts [from pp. 42-346] of *Learning to Love: The Journals
of Thomas Merton, Volume Six 1966-1967* by Thomas Merton and edited
by Christine Bochen, copyright © 1997 by The Merton Legacy Trust, are
reprinted by permission of HarperCollins Publishers.

Published by In Extenso Press
Distributed exclusively by ACTA Publications, 4848 N. Clark Street,
Chicago, IL 60640, (800) 397-2282, actapublications.com

Library of Congress Catalog Number: 2014937626
ISBN: 978-0-87946-997-9
Printed in the United States of America by Total Printing Systems
Year 25 24 23 22 21 20 19 18 17 16 15 14
Printing 15 14 13 12 11 10 9 8 7 6 5 4 3 2

✪ Text printed on 30% post-consumer recycled paper

CONTENTS

INTRODUCTION

*It is impossible for the human heart
to be opened from outside;
and then someone comes along
and does just that.*

I woke up one night with the words in my mind. I assumed they came from my subconscious. I immediately got up and wrote them down, knowing that they were to be significant in whatever came later, should I ever take up the story of Thomas Merton and the woman he referred to in his journal only as "M." These words seemed to me to capture the paradox of intimacy: that in one way it is essential to decide to allow people into our private life; in another way, that entry can only come from another's insisting presence. The paper on which I wrote these words had been sitting on my writing table for a long time—collecting dust, getting wrinkled and faded, while I kept putting off writing what I now offer for your consideration.

This is a book I knew I must write, although I resisted doing so for several years. My reasons for avoiding this task were several. The first was my usual hesitancy—and that of many who write—around my having nothing of importance to say on the subject, of evaluating myself as unqualified to speak on what I wanted to address. Another concern I had was the complexity of the relationship, which baffled Merton and on which he went back and forth in his thinking, feelings, and actions. Who was I to think any commentary of mine would expand and enlighten his own clear and eloquent—if often contradictory—words?

How was I to penetrate—presumably more deeply than he had—the relationship with a woman about twenty-five years his junior, about which he wrote so much and left so little unsaid?

However, several people who knew Merton personally and have read my previous book on Merton and the Enneagram, (*Merton, An Enneagram Profile*), have commented how well I seem to intuit thoughts and feelings he had only revealed to his closest friends. Since they knew I never met Merton personally they wondered how this level of understanding is possible. One of those people, Charles Dumont, in his review of my book in the periodical *Collectanea Cisterciensa*, attributed this phenomenon both to Merton's and my common monastic background as well as the dynamics of the number four personality on the Enneagram that Thomas Merton and I share. Whatever the reason for my insights, these assurances that my statements about Merton resonate with those closest to him have encouraged me to write further. While I did touch on his relationship with Margie in my previous book, I want to focus on this exclusively in this set of reflections.

Merton's journal refers to Margie simply as "M." (See *Learning to Love.* Note: All references to books will be by the initials of their title, followed by page numbers based on the editions listed in "Resources" at the end.) We know from other sources that her name was Margie and that a few Merton confidants know her complete identity. She would be in her seventies now.

To me, all these questions of her real identity and current whereabouts are irrelevant to my purpose here, which is to use Merton's own writings (real and imagined) about her to reflect on their relationship back then and its meaning to us today.

Who was this woman, and how did he, at the age of fifty-one, only two years before he died in a tragic accident while on a journey to Asia, find her stopping him in his spiritual tracks?

Margie was a young nurse in her mid-twenties when they met. Merton had been hospitalized for back surgery and she was appointed to care for him. Margie had been for a short time in a religious community. Because of that, we can assume she had read some of Merton's writings and was most likely impressed by the man she met in the hospital ward. Merton was, of course , already quite famous. His book *The Seven Storey Mountain* had sold millions of copies and was considered one of the greatest spiritual books of the time. He was now unwell and in pain and undoubtedly on medications that might have lowered his instinctive emotional defenses with a young, attractive, unmarried woman. In addition, Merton appears to have been ready for the relationship. He had written, reflecting on this hospitalization, that he was experiencing a lack of connection with the feminine in his life and saw that fact as a limitation in his personality.

The very subject of Merton's journal entries on his relationship with Margie has always been controversial. This, too, gave me pause. There are some people (I know, I have met several) who have lost respect for Merton because of this issue. I guess they feel that he was unfaithful to his vows, at least in spirit, by even entertaining a love for a real, flesh-and-blood woman. They think him weak at best and hypocritical at worst. And they are even offended that he should even write about his feelings in a "spiritual" journal.

There are others, like me, who believed that his relationship with Margie was important, even essential, for him to become a complete human being. When I heard of Merton's accidental death, electrocuted by a faulty fan after taking a bath in Thailand in 1968, I remarked to many people that to me he seemed not yet ready to die. My reason at the time was that in my estimation his writing on spirituality had become for some years before his death more and more distant and inaccessible: drier, more esoteric, more cerebral, less relevant. Only when his journal *Learning to Love* was published—over twenty-five years after his death—did I become convinced of the timeliness of his dying. For in that journal he revealed how vulnerable, how out of control, how wildly and immaturely romantic—and therefore how human—he could be. Because of his love for Margie, I now believe, Merton finally became *incarnate*, that is, a "spirit in flesh" —as all followers of Jesus of Nazareth, the original "Word made flesh," are called to become. As Jesus was not afraid to become "one of us," neither any longer was Merton after he met Margie. With her, and apparently only her, he was ready to risk discovering more deeply than ever the inevitable imperfections of his humanity while trusting completely in the mercy and love of God for him...and for us.

Another question I had around writing on this topic concerned how willing people might be, in the face of scandals around sexuality and priesthood today, to accept that Merton had found himself open to so intimate a relationship. This concern is why I, a vowed religious woman, have chosen the approach you find in this book of imagining what Merton might have felt and writing it in a poem at the beginning of each chapter. Rather than giving my intellectual assessment of Merton or critiquing his relationship with Margie in these imagined poems, I have attempted to summarize aspects of Merton's spiritual struggle in what I present as his own voice. I cannot tell you what an artistic risk I feel I am taking in doing so. Who am I to pretend to write what I think Merton might have written? I do so in a spirit of humility, only because I could not think of any other way to get to the heart of the matter. I feel that I understand what Merton was going through, not only because of what he wrote in his journal but also because of what so many have gone through in the own struggle to understand what it means to love.

I hope these imagined poems, the real quotes from Merton, and my brief commentaries on the various issues Merton confronted in trying to understand and respond to his and Margie's love for each other can help you focus on your own lovability and love for others. His comments on his relationship with Margie cut through his journal of this period, including the diary he sent to Margie in 1966 (see *Midsummer Diary for M*, LTL, 303-348). I encourage you to read them for yourself and draw your own conclusions and lessons.

All I want to do here is to do the same thing myself, with sensitivity to the pain and struggle his situation with Margie obviously caused Merton. To accomplish this task, and after trying several possibilities of how to address the challenge, I have chosen the following format: First, I start with a poem that I wrote in the imagined voice of Thomas Merton; second, I offer an actual quote from Merton; third, I offer my own short reflections on both the poem and the quote.

It seems to me there are a few salient arguments Merton grappled with that come out of the many pages of his journal from this time in his life. Because I trust that I somehow understand Merton's process, and because—as I have noted previously—I have been supported in that trust, I have attempted to focus his mental meanderings in a style similar to his journal entries. These short entries are my attempt to articulate the various aspects of his love for Margie and his struggle around them. They are not chronological but rather thematic. Though it was not my plan when I began to compose these reflections, there have turned out to be eighteen of them, the same number as the poems Merton wrote about Margie during this time (Merton, *Eighteen Poems*). While this number was coincidental, I simply mention it as being of interest to me and perhaps to you.

I still present this book with much trepidation. How do I

dare compose what I think Thomas Merton would have written about a woman whose identity we don't really know? What leads me to believe my approach adds anything to his own eloquent reflections? Most importantly for me, how might Merton himself respond to my putting words into his mouth? I can only answer those concerns by saying that I have long searched for a way to speak about this time in his life, one which I consider very significant. What follows here is the only way I know how to respond to the requests I have had to put my insights into written form. Please take them for what they are worth, in the spirit in which they are offered.

With this introduction, then, I present what I hope will be artistic, but true at the deepest level, reflections on the relationship of Merton with the woman he loved. In my opinion, it was Margie, more than any other person or any other experience, who brought the spiritual master to embrace the fullness of his humanity.

I hope what follows in these pages will at least be a clear articulation of how Merton faced and grappled with the questions of personal integrity and vocational commitment in his intimate relationship with a woman. At best, my hope is that my book helps clarify the personality of a man who was ahead of his time in so many ways, yet only learned near the very end of his life that the ground of love and truth lies not in the abstract but in the physical reality of other human beings.

Over the years in my work as a psychotherapist and spiritual director, I have come to know that people in the contemporary world and in the church privately address these questions. *Learning to Love* is a volume Merton allowed—even intended—to be published. In his prophetic way he anticipated and chose to articulate some of the issues celibate women and men religious face. Whether he foresaw what might come of his openness we do not know. What we do know is that he let us hear his honest statements around them and the decisions he made. Once again, in this final aspect of his life, Merton has touched people in our time as we try in our own lives to discover what it means to be committed creatures of the Creator and followers of Jesus Christ. If this book contributes in any way to making one person better understand what it means to be fully human, I will be satisfied. When you have read the following pages, you can determine for yourself whether I have succeeded in doing so.

I

I've always believed in incarnation,
But I think I haven't lived it much;
Maybe only in an occasional
Burst of some pious bubble
Blown up by me or somebody else
That says,
Let's get real. Let's write real.
But now
Let's live real is a door I'm not allowed to
Open.
But that contradicts my incarnation.
You only know how much is enough
By knowing how much is too much.
Deserts have no paths.
Risk has to be; where else grows wisdom?
But not in this arena?
This sounds insane
Any way you cut it.
Nuts if you plunge into it, into her.
Nuts if you wall off this fire at its Source.
At the body, the soul,
The all of me.

Thomas Merton did write:

Genuine love is a personal revolution. Love takes your ideas, your desires, and your actions and welds them together in one experience and one living reality which is a new you. (*Love and Living*, 28)

. . . .

I now write:

When I first read this quotation from Thomas Merton's book *Love and Living*, I assumed he was talking about his relationship with God. Surely it could have had meaning if applied that way. Later on, however, I found that he had already experienced his relationship with Margie, the woman he always referred to in his journal only as "M," when he wrote these words. And I, like Merton, believe them to be true of all situations. We are used to words like "transformation" to describe the depth of the change that love can make in us if and when we leave ourselves open to receive it. Someone who risks this openness will never be the same again.

Merton's thesis here is that love takes you out of yourself, that you must fall into love, risking security and soundness for something "stronger than reason and more imperious even than business." (LAL, 26)

Coolness and self-possession will have to go in the face of real love, and a certain silliness is inevitable. One has to become something of a fool to allow the vulnerability necessitated by love on all levels of our existence. Merton speaks about how people in love's emotions take over, even disturbing their eating and drinking and sleeping. Anyone who has ever yielded to love knows this to be true.

But the heart of the experience of love is more than the making of something ridiculous. It is, Merton tells us, our human destiny. Only when we can give ourselves over to someone in the way of love can we experience "a wholeness, a fullness of life." (*LAL*, 27)

Love is, of course, more than romance, although it can certainly include this component—as it does for so many. True love, according to Merton, embraces all of ourselves: "the capacity for self-giving, for sharing, for creativity, for mutual care, for spiritual concern."

> *We do not find the meaning of life by ourselves alone—we find it with another. We do not discover the secret of our lives merely by study and calculation in our own isolated meditations. The meaning of our life is a secret that has to be revealed to us in love, by the one we love. And if this love is unreal, the secret will not be found, the meaning will never reveal itself, the message will never be decoded.... We will never be fully real until we let ourselves fall in love— either with another human person or with God. (LAL, 27)*

The question that remains for me is whether human, romantic love is essential for the fullness of the experience of love. This may well be the question that always remained for Merton. Can a human being really learn the life-lessons of love without the intervention of another person with whom one is completely open and vulnerable? Whatever other people might decide is the correct answer to this question—and Merton leaves it open for others to resolve—for him the response is clear. Nothing before his relationship with Margie had convinced him that he was lovable. And nothing after their relationship began was needed to prove to him that he was lovable. Michael Mott, Merton's official biographer, tells us that, after his experience of Margie, Merton never again talked of his inability to love and be loved. (Mott, 438)

Clearly for Merton, a human being—a young nurse about twenty-five years his junior—was the way God used to allow him to finally lose control and embrace his human vulnerability:

> *My true meaning and worth are shown to me not in my estimate of myself, but in the eyes of the one who loves me; and that one must love me as I am, with my faults and limitations, revealing to me the truth that these faults and limitations cannot destroy my worth in their eyes; and that I am therefore valuable as a person, in spite of my shortcomings, in spite of the imperfections of my exterior "package." (LAL, 35)*

II

Thomas Merton might have written:

What worth is my monastic call
If I deny my human one?
Granted, I should have seen all this
Years ago.
But it didn't happen.
Probably because my sight was bad
Probably too because of circumstances.
It's only now that it's here
To be admitted.
My false self will only torture me
By laughing a monstrous laugh
At my real me.
So here goes; here it is:
I'm a middle-aged monk
Acting like a teenager and
The only way out
Is through.

Thomas Merton did write:

April 27, 1966

My response has been too total and too forthright, we have admitted too much, communicated all the fire to each other and now we are caught. I am not as smart or as stable as I imagined. (LTL, 46)

. . . .

I now write:

It would seem to me that Margie—or some other human being with warmth similar to hers—would have had, of necessity for his spiritual development, to find a way into Merton's life. Apparently, this great spiritual writer had never had an experience of true human love for a woman, with all of its physical, emotional, psychological, and spiritual aspects. He goes on to say in his journal a few days later that it would need to be in mutuality that such learning would take place: "I see one thing only: to go on hesitantly, perhaps, but trustingly trying to answer the demands of this deep personal commitment to her in love, to really, deeply return her love...." (LTL, 51)

By the time he met Margie, Merton had lived for decades in his Cistercian monastery; and he had not found, until Margie crossed his path, anything in his life to match her effect on him. It is true that over the years of his monastic commitment Merton's devotion to Mary, the Mother of God, had grown in his personal prayer life and had been articulated in some of his writings. Nevertheless, as he described in his journal, he had become increasingly aware that, despite his prayerful relationship with the woman who bore Jesus, something very primal, very essential, was missing in his development.

Margie's overtures of physical care as she attended to Merton's needs related to his recovery from a back operation touched him. She also was able to share with him on something of an intellectual level, since she had read and appreciated some of his ideas. They met at a time of Merton's growing awareness of his lack of feminine love and realization of his stunted emotional maturity. He uses the image of being "torn open" when he finally admits his profound need for the companionship and love of a woman. (LTL, 38)

In Margie, he foresees there may be a remedy for his loneliness and isolation. In fact, the remedy is described in the same image; her love tears him open and he sees her as filling up that cavernous emptiness he has only recently become aware of. (LTL, 46)

Merton's consciousness of his human need for real love clearly caused him great pain. He realized the risk he would have to take if he were to respond to Margie's overtures of friendship. He spoke of the "courtesy" she deserved as a response for her expressed interest in him. What a strange way of putting it! It was much more than "courtesy" that both Margie and he longed for. To his credit, Merton acknowledged very early on that he was not merely dispensing Christian kindness to Margie. He was not in some position of power where this relationship was concerned. He had become infatuated, there is no doubt about that. While he feared he would have to explore a place in his psyche that he had left unattended and undeveloped, he judged it necessary—for his own sake—to pursue the relationship no matter where it took him. He seemed to understand that only the experience of real, human love could teach him what he desperately needed to learn.

III

• Thomas Merton might have written:

I'm no expert
God knows
At anything,
Certainly not at this:
This crazy surge of something
For want of a better word
I call "love"
That makes me feel so young
And foolish.
When I'm down on myself
I sneer at
Ridiculous me
For riding a midlife motorcycle.
But when mercy comes back
I know there is love in it all
Of God, of me, and of her—
Yes, surely of her—
Beneath accusations
Of wrongdoing
That are unjust
And violate both of us
And God, too.

Thomas Merton did write:

April 28, 1966

It seems like a contradiction of all I have been striving for and writing about...and living for. Somehow I know it isn't. Yet I have no way of rationalizing that one! I will just have to leave it as it is—vulnerable and ridiculous.... Groping for support and strength—where else but in God's word. (LTL, 47-48)

. . . .

I now write:

If I were to select the major theme in the early springtime months of Merton's 1966 journal, it would be his conviction that somehow—no matter how things looked to others and sometimes to himself—there was rightness in his relationship with Margie. That certainty was fundamental, one which he could not deny except to violate his own conscience. This leads us, as it did him, to the question as to what he considered the basic underpinning for his—and Margie's—decisions about what to do about their new-found feelings for each other.

Priority for Merton in this matter was certainly not given to the monastic law or his religious vows. His concern was to discern what was life-giving for both of them in this situation. This does not mean that he dismissed the law or his vows. Had that been the case, he would not have experienced the constant ambiguity that surrounded his increasing involvement with Margie, which can be found on nearly every page of the journal of this period. He seemed to find the relationship inexplicable, given who he was and the life choices he had made. On the other hand, he felt himself to be alive in a way that was not only new but also necessary. He seemed to understand on a visceral level that without Margie, he could never become a full human being… and that with her he would. Nevertheless, as someone who had written so knowledgeably about following the false self, he could not help but ask if he was deluding himself, and possibly Margie as well.

> …*I know that in itself this love is a thing of enormous value (never has anyone given herself to me so completely, so openly, so frankly, and never have I responded so completely). Yet it is in absolute conflict with every social canon, feeling, predetermination etc. and* everyone, *the pious and the feisty, will use it for one thing only—to crush and discredit us.* (LTL, 47)

Here we see Merton not so much considering the morality of his actions before God but rather how others would judge Margie and him. His defensiveness as he thinks about their being judged is evident, as is his anger at those he feels would never realize the importance of their relationship and the angst it causes both of them. For Merton, the urgency of following where his and Margie's relationship will take them gains precedence over anything else, and most certainly over any potential or perceived damage to his reputation or that of the monastery. In his defiance, he seems to be choosing what he thinks important for the two of them, whatever the consequences might turn out to be.

When all is said and done, Merton decides to obey what he considers the radical imperative of his true self and simply love

Margie. He cannot in conscience end what they have begun. In his journal, he moves on, giving himself increasingly to Margie and his relationship with her: "All I can think of is to pray for her as earnestly and honestly as possible and leave the rest to God." (LTL, 49)

IV

Merton might have written:

Something has been missing
All these years.
I wonder if this is the only way
To find it,
Especially since I'm not even sure
What it is.
Lonely, untouched, certain
And secure:
That describes me pretty well
Until now when
With her warmth she touches me all over
Inside and out.
And I hope it will never end and
I don't care if I'm
A fool.

Merton did write:

May 10, 1966

I am myself. I do not make myself, or bring myself into conformity with some nonsensical ideal. One of the good things about this love is seeing myself as loved by M. True, she idealizes me impossibly, yet at the same time unavoidably I am known to her as I am and many of the things she loves in me are things I find humiliating and impossible. But she loves them because they are concretely mine, and I love her in the same way. This surely is a very good thing! (LTL, 58)

. . . .

I now write:

In early May of 1966, Merton began his love poems to Margie. Eventually there were eighteen of these, some of which are included in his journal, *Learning to Love*. He realized that she had somehow found a way around his tendency toward inner withdrawal, and this continually amazed him. Although he was outgoing and even gregarious in the presence of people, Merton's loneliness and isolation were a very real underlying experience for him. It would seem that he had always feared someone might learn to know him well—and if they did see who he really was they would surely discover his humiliating faults and, very rightly, abandon him. By holding people off, he maintained a safe, predictable existence, even though it meant distancing himself from who he really was and what he really felt. Merton had thought all his life that if he ever allowed anyone to come too close to him the person would consider him a fraud. As he says in the above passage, however, with Margie he experienced quite the opposite, and "this surely is a very good thing."

Margie proved him wrong. She accepted him in all his imperfections, be they of body or of spirit; she had demonstrated that to be so. And he marveled at her awareness of the truth of him. He was also amazed that he could let himself be open so freely in response to her. He acknowledged "that the deepest capacities for human love in me have never even been tapped, that I too can love with an awful completeness." (LTL, 54)

What was Thomas Merton to do, having found awakened this profoundly significant part of himself that had remained almost completely undeveloped until now? Could he allow to be buried again what was so vital to his being not only fully human but truly Christian as well? If the Christ-life that he had aspired to since his conversion and entering the monastery meant affirming and expressing the oneness of all people (a world in which all barriers to love have been dissolved), then how could he continue to write about such things without living what he was saying when it came to Margie? She had made him acutely aware that he had never been completely open with other people, never been his entire self with them. His relationships had always been guarded—at least, it seems, emotionally. Margie had shown him what openness to another human being must mean and that he needed to let all aspects of himself be known—at least to someone he truly loved and who loved him in the same way. He had come to realize that there were essential life lessons to be learned by doing so—lessons that every monk, every vowed religious, every Christian, indeed every human needs to understand and act upon.

Merton had been trying over and over again to address the

questions of the true nature of love, even before Margie entered his life. Each time he would do so differently. On the one hand he believed Christianity was a call to freedom and wholeness, which he had always judged to be the purpose of human, and therefore Christian, existence; Margie had made him realize what that might involve. On the other hand, Merton felt a concrete responsibility to continue on the life path he had freely chosen and still valued; yet he was now realizing that might mean doing so without the companionship of the one person who had revealed to him the true nature of the Way.

> *A voice says in me—love; do trust love! Do not fear it, do not avoid it, do not take mere half-measures with it, but love, believe in it, without any special program, without rebelling against the whole structure of the church, without ignoring or neglecting (or idolizing) concrete obligations which you may have, but* love *within the actual framework where you are and see what comes of it. This must mean a great freedom of spirit in regard to a lot of things and even a certain flexibility with regard to some monastic rules. (But my own suspicion says: where can it ever get you?) (LTL, 57)*

Merton faced a paradox: could he love without loving Margie? And this is not the last time his analysis of his situation had come around to the same questions with which it began. In the face of the paradox, he just gave up trying to figure things out, hoping answers would eventually be revealed, answers that somehow would include Margie as part of them. If his journal readers today are sometimes bored or exasperated with his circular thinking, he seemed to become bored himself with the obsessive attempts to come down on one side or the other regarding his love for Margie. But obsessive as it all was, he could not let this struggle go. He was pulled in both directions without resolution. At least at the beginning....

V

Women aren't strangers to me.
I've had my share—
And I know that sounds disgustingly male.
I've been just friends with others
In various ways, each different.
But vulnerable like this
Never.
My iron walls are melted down
By her cool care
And I'm here naked
Like who I really am
And have been always
And never let anyone see
Even myself.
There's a wound she's touched
That's not been healed
Ever,
And my guts tremble
In what I can call either
Pain or ecstasy.
I'm not sure which.
Maybe it's love.
I wouldn't know.
How could I?
This is
Trackless territory.

Merton did write:

April 19, 1966

The question of love: I have to face the fact that I have simply side-stepped it. Now it must be faced squarely. I cannot live without giving love back to a world that has given me so much. And of course it has to be the love of a man dedicated to God—and selfless, detached, free, completely open love. And I have not attained to such a level, hence the risk. (LTL, 42)

. . . .

I now write:

Merton has been accused of being something of a male chauvinist. Someone I know used the old-fashioned word "cad" to describe him. A part of Merton, in his more honest moments, might accept that accusation. In his autobiography, *The Seven Storey Mountain*, he speaks of relationships with women in his Cambridge University days with distance and disengagement. His sexual encounters there were self-admittedly perfunctory; they were activities by which he defined an image of himself he was trying to create at that time in his life. The word "love" seems not to have been part of his consideration, his understanding, or his value system. Rather, he seemed in these affairs to be somewhat deliberately building for himself—and probably for others—the identity of a male with sexual prowess as one of the defining characteristics of "Thomas Merton." (As a counselor, I would say that the social milieu in which he circulated probably contributed to this being the case.)

His Columbia University years, however, led to a re-shuffling of values for Merton and culminated in his conversion to Catholicism and decision to enter religious life, first as a Franciscan and later as a Trappist. During his university years he did have women friends who might be best seen as companions, almost pals. They were part of the group he traveled with in graduate school and beyond. He speaks of them as significant friends, but the sexual aspects of relationships with them did not become a priority for him. For one thing, his professional life demanded much of his attention, especially as he began to teach full time. At this period he writes repeatedly in his journal about his readings in various spiritual traditions and the variety of ways to pray. It seems that he was so involved in his personal vocational discernment that all else took a back seat to that.

After he entered Gethsemani and became famous for his autobiography and a series of books on spirituality, there were other women moving in and out of his life. There were those who helped him publish his writings, assisted with some administrative details of his increasingly busy life, or engaged with him around issues of vowed religious life and the formation of new men and women religious. And, of course, there was always his writing and other social and monastic concerns in which women became interested and involved.

This is not to say that his relationships with women were insignificant. Some of these women were certainly important to him, and he expressed his gratitude often for them...and to them as well. Some of the women he perhaps "used" at times, in the sense that they did something for him that he needed to have done, sometimes without much recognition or gratitude on his part. Other women clearly challenged his thinking and forced him to articulate his beliefs.

But as important as these relationships were to him, Merton knew they never forced him to be vulnerable. The wound that had convinced him of his unlovableness had been dealt many years before by a woman, his mother. I am not going to go into this aspect of Merton's personality here, but his relationship with her has been well-documented, both by him and by others.

Suffice it to say that Merton eventually came to an awareness that he was wounded in this aspect of his life, and that a woman would need to heal it. He talks about something being missing in his life in his journal of 1966 in what reads like a foreshadowing. He was ready for an inner void in his ability to love to be filled, and Margie stepped in—almost on cue—to make that happen.

Merton rather quickly opened himself on all levels to Margie. When he did so, he experienced the inevitable effect of complete, naked vulnerability: a rush of ecstasy that is so intense as to be painful. As Richard Rohr says in *Immortal Diamond*:

> *It should be no scandal or surprise that sex is so obsessive, scary, and fascinating. It is the most dramatic way we all try to overcome our separateness.... Even our clumsy amorous attempts give us a taste and a promise now and then, and there is not much point in always calling them "sins."* (Rohr, 101)

Rohr goes on to say that "God is not going to waste anything and will use everything, even those clumsy amorous attempts, to bring us into union with God and ourselves." (Rohr, 101)

Merton seemed to sense that to be true. He loved Margie, or so he honestly believed and declared to himself repeatedly in his journal entries. He speaks about also telling her of his love. Somehow he seems confident that this love for her must have some connection with the love of God for him and he for God, since it resulted in his accepting his own goodness. He experienced love-made-real through her person. He had few words to explain how that could be, but he was certain it was true. Thomas Merton repeatedly named Margie's love for him as the avenue for his late-blooming awareness of his own goodness.

Merton struggled to walk the line between the physical expression of their love and the spiritual significance he knew it had for him and, as he hoped in his journal, also for Margie:

> *I do so much want to love her as we began, spiritually—I do believe such spiritual love is not only possible but does exist between us, deeply, purely, strongly, and the rest can be controlled. Yet she is right to be scared. We can simply wreck each other. I am determined not to give in to this, not to yield to fear and despair, to keep it on a level where it belongs, but I can see I really don't know how to handle this if it ever breaks loose. (LTL, 46)*

The relationship with Margie seemed completely contradictory to everything Merton had ever learned was acceptable for any vowed religious, but he was convinced he had to proceed, even though he could not find any intellectual theory to lend support to the path he was on with her. As with the doctrinal mysteries in which he had put his faith, so he was sure he must embrace this mystery and keep going...or else be unfaithful to what was his inner truth.

VI

Merton might have written:

The surest voice I hear
Is this: I am a monk
Forever.
Lying here in the dark silence
Is another truth: I want her and
I need her.
So now what?
This bed holds both of me;
But wait a minute.
Beside these two parts of me
She rests.
All of a sudden
My alarm goes off
And I wake up and wish
I were free.
But for what? For which?
It rings out
"You're never too old
To choose again."
That's the end of sleep.

Merton did write:

May 9, 1966

*A voice says in me—love: do trust love! Do not fear it, do
not avoid it, do not take mere half-measures with it, but
love, believe in it, without any special program, without
rebelling against the whole structure of the church, without
ignoring or neglecting (or idolizing) concrete obligations
which you may have, but love within the actual framework
where you are and see what comes of it. (LTL, 57)*

. . . .

I now write:

I assume, since Merton had written about his insomnia in an
earlier journal, that the situation with Margie would have
kept him awake sometimes at night; hence, the image I used
in his imagined poem above. On the one hand, the answer to
Merton's entire dilemma was a simple one: Many years earlier he
had made a permanent decision for Cistercian monastic life in
the monastery at Gethsemani. This involved, of course, a vow of
"chastity," as it was called in Merton's time (now more usually referred to as "celibacy," which is understood as a promise to refrain
from sexual relations of any kind). Another specifically monastic
vow is *conversatio morum*, best translated, according to scholars,
as "fidelity to the monastic way of life." These dual vows consti-
tuted a double deterrent to any consideration of a relationship
with Margie that was anything other than platonic.

What Merton had promised—to himself, to God, and to

the world—in this regard was quite clear to him and, apparently from what he writes at this time, never before seriously questioned. While it is true that Merton had entertained and even pursued the possibility of transferring to another monastery, leaving monastic life entirely had never seemed to be a consideration for him. The relationship with Margie made things clearly different. Merton was faced with the necessity of making a second vocational decision, one which he never thought he would entertain and one he did not think he could make without denying his earlier monastic one. But in his journal he seriously wonders whether looking at his monastic choice as irrevocable is truly the loving thing to do in the new situation he finds himself with Margie. Perhaps her presence in his life was a sign that God was leading him beyond his present vowed commitment to one of another kind?

At this period in the 1960s, a number of women and men religious were choosing to leave religious life. The climate in church renewal during and after Vatican II was allowing new questions and reassessments around older traditions, among them those of what "lifetime" vows might actually mean in changing times. "Chastity" was something expected of everyone according to his or her vocational state. Celibacy, on the other hand, was now often being described as some kind of "non-marriage for the kingdom." Could this new definition of his original vow offer Merton a broader view of where Margie might fit into his life? Might they even find some place for sexuality in their relationship without marrying? Could he be committed to his vowed life as well as to her, or should he just admit that he could not fulfill the promise he had made in good faith, leave the religious life as so many others were doing, marry Margie, and "live happily ever after"? That question became the source of others for Merton around how practical it would be for them to continue their relationship.

It would be a difficult tightrope to walk, but he and she kept on exploring the possibility of doing so.

On May 9, he writes in his journal: "I am struck by the fact that the social rules of thumb for handling such situations offer no real structure, no authentic answer, and one cannot begin to make sense of norms!" He talks about just leaving and "living together 'married,'" but by putting that word in quotation marks he seems to say that even thinking about such a solution makes no sense to him. (LTL, 54-55)

Merton is enough of a traditionalist that going through the proper church channels to gain a dispensation from his vows immediately rises up as important. And besides, given his reputation in the church as a monk and spiritual leader, he surely felt that being dispensed from his vows would be difficult, time-consuming, and perhaps impossible. Would the authorities even entertain his leaving religious life with permission? These were some of the issues Merton grappled with at the time.

The Hamlet-like interior dialogue continued as he talked about the necessary "legal machinery" of the dispensation process and wondered: "It claims to be the voice of God, it pretends to damn in His name and by His authority...Does it really? Is it a mark of faith to accept this in timid fear, so that one closes his mind in desperation to all other more intimate and more personal values?" Merton offered no answer to these questions, but he pointed out that they should be "seriously asked in this time after Vatican II." (LTL, 55)

Small relief for him and Margie in their very real situation, and one has to wonder what she thought about his dithering!

This particular back and forth about seeking a dispensation from vows and leaving religious life closed with no conclusion but an attitude that is not definitive: "It is, however, now, to me, a really serious option: that if in the near future the way *does* open for a married clergy, I should take it." (LTL, 55)

This seems to be the only possibility and the only consolation Merton could think of—not a very helpful one, given the immediacy of his and Margie's relationship.

VII

Merton might have written:

We're free of the law
St. Paul says.
But I've not lived like I
Believe that
Until now,
And even now
Not entirely,
Not all the time,
But only in a few moments
Strung like bright beads
On the dull chain
I call my life;
A sort of rosary
I finger and pray
When she's not here.
Love is the law
Now.
Love and do what you will.
Augustine said that.
Soothing, brave words
That hold truth.
But another guy, Pilate, asked
What is truth?

Merton did write:

May 28, 1966

I must give everything I have to my real task. Love for M is not incompatible with that task but it has to be left on a certain level. One on which both of us are helped, taught, grow, deepen, and do not squander ourselves absurdly, as we tend to do.

If our love can teach us this, then we will certainly gain by it immensely. (LTL, 71-72)

. . . .

I now write:

The question of what love and truth really are is asked repeatedly throughout Merton's journal of this period. For him, there is now something of a radical purity called for in what he now names "love" with Margie. While we see him here in many ways almost blindly exuberant about being known by and knowing Margie, he does retain a basic honesty as he assesses what has developed between them.

He writes, "Of course I am not detached and neither is she. We are profoundly and firmly attached to each other. I am more aware of it all the time because my nature at times rebels against being 'held' like this." This kind of openness and vulnerability from Merton are new at the time, and they seem to reveal to him the depth to which he had allowed himself to be touched by Margie. He realizes how much power Margie holds over him, and it is a power he has gladly allowed her to have. He is not always sure he should have let this happen, however. He goes on to say "We are far beyond the point where I used to get off the bus in all my old love affairs. I am in much deeper than I ever was before." (LTL, 75)

Merton is finally struck by a sensitivity toward the women he had relationships with in college (and perhaps felt now that he had taken advantage of). He adds this comment to his journal in parentheses: "In the light of M's love I realize for the first time how deeply I was loved back in those days by girls whose names I have even forgotten." (LTL, 75)

In effect, the delicate respect for a specific woman he experiences with Margie draws forth in him a new respect for other women he has known and, by extension at least, all women. Because of Margie's love for him, Merton became aware of the love his youthful sexual partners may have had for him and experienced sorrow for his lack of real love in these encounters. I believe that this regret and even guilt on his part was both real and healthy. This is why I say he *had* to encounter Margie, or someone like her, in order to truly come to understand truth and love before his unexpected and sudden death.

The word "love," which Merton in my opinion had used flippantly throughout his career, has taken on a new sacredness. As for many of us whose experience and, therefore, definition of love have deepened to the point of visceral comprehension of its power, St. Augustine's famous exhortation to "love and do what you will" can no longer be seen as superficial permission to be hedonistic. Love, when it is experienced at its deepest level between people, takes on aspects of a profound call to what Merton calls "sacrifices." He adds about his love for Margie: "This love is a disconcerting, risky, hard-to-handle reality. But it is 'real.'" (LTL, 77)

Multiple times in his journal, Merton warns himself against theorizing about love, concentrating on the "essence of love" or the "essence of woman." Margie is a "concrete, existing woman who gives herself to me as she is." (LTL, 77)

Disengaged and objective are not possible for him any longer; love is now a concrete person named Margie.

The question continued to remain for Merton, however, as to how completely this presence of Margie is to be experienced, on what levels of mind and body they can give themselves to one another. Where does the truth of their love, now that he appreciates what it genuinely is, end? What can love mean for them, given not only its reality but also the reality of their individual circumstances? He is a *monk*, and a famous one at that! She is his *nurse*, and about twenty-five years his junior! He talks about where they stand in early June of 1966 and says of Margie and himself:

> ...*she asks a love that fully respects her in her wholeness as person (this does not exclude sex by any means, but in our case circumstances do—what is important is the union of which sex is only a sign). I have to stop making sex a problem in this (torment, wanting it so badly and knowing it has to remain impossible, fear of going into it in some messy dishonest way)! (LTL, 77)*

Merton sent Margie his *Midsummer Diary for M* that year, and in it he not only speaks directly to her at times but also allows her into his thoughts about the two of them in parts written in journal style. In this latter approach he sees himself as writing "much more sanely" (LTL, 126) because he is not merely turning ideas around in his own head, but sharing them with her. In support of his assessment about being more truthful when he includes her as a witness to his words, he says with simple directness:

The real desert is this: to face the real limitations of one's own existence and knowledge and not try to manipulate them or disguise them. Not to embellish them with possibilities. To simply set aside all possibilities other than those that are actually present and real, here and now. And then to choose or not, as one wishes, knowing that no choice is a solution to anything but merely a step further into a slightly changed context of other, very few, very limited, very meaningless concrete possibilities. (LTL, 309-310)

As most of us have learned the hard way, this kind of real, honest, physical love can occur in anyone's life, and it helps us understand what love is in a truthful and honest way. The difference with Merton is that he is so introspective and so dedicated to the spiritual search that he would, of course, write down every thought on the subject, no matter how personal or painful it might be. Most of us, if we did this, would have our diaries or journals thrown in the trash by our unsuspecting (or perhaps wise) relatives; Merton's reflections were published for all to see.

Merton goes on to say, as a lifetime of searching for self-knowledge has taught him, that "analyzing and rationalizing are of very little help. With me this can easily be a vice." (LTL, 332)

And so, reaching for straightforward honesty that he knows from experience can elude him, the question that Pilate posed to Jesus about the nature of truth becomes Merton's own. What does loving Margie truthfully mean? More importantly, what does it require of him if he is to stay true to the Christian command to love (despite or because of whatever "permanent" vow one might have taken)? Are he and Margie somehow to build a life together, or is that impossible? And if it is impossible, what then? These emerge as Merton's most frequently occurring questions as their relationship intensifies.

VIII

Merton might have written:

There's death in my heart
Or maybe my brain.
It's perfectly logical this can't be.
Such a sensible thought
Sounds sterile
To me, and surely to her.
Where is the life here
For either of us,
Two chilled corpses?
God can't bless this
Death of vibrant, hot flesh.
And if he does, he's not the God
I can follow anymore.
To hell with going back
To what once was.
To hell with the God who is not
Life itself.
To hell with me?

Merton did write:

June of 1966

To be a monk is to be forever neutral. At least with respect to certain incidentals like life, love, despair, anguish. (But of course we have our home-made anguish, too. It keeps us out of mischief. That is the plan for me: return to the habit of neutral anguish, a life lived by quiet custom, according to precise specifications.) (LTL, 305)

. . . .

I now write:

These words above, from Merton's *Midsummer Diary for M,* were written for Margie in June of 1966. They feel heavy with depression in the most concrete definition of that word. His spirit is pressed down, and he sounds as if he can see only a necessary withdrawing from the feelings Margie has enkindled in him and that he has come to see as essential for his ability to live a full and mature life. He sees no way out for this future except to suppress the totally human response to Margie he has come to believe is true love. And he seems to blame monasticism for imposing this life-draining solution, not only on him but on her. Not only does he appear certain that his feelings of vulnerability with her will be lost if he is to remain a monk, but he apparently believes he will even lose touch with his negative emotions, such as despair and anguish as well. These feelings, too, as the journal testifies, he had experienced as a part of his loving relationship with Margie. If intensity was the name of the game in his love for Margie, then Merton could only foresee a flat and barren future ahead when and if he returned to his former life and the monastic routine. And returning to them looked at times like the only sensible path.

Not only is Merton saddened; he is also angry. Read this passage again: "(But of course we have our home-made anguish, too. It keeps us out of mischief. That is the plan for me: return to the habit of neutral anguish, a life lived by quiet custom, according to precise specifications.)" Even the fact that he put these words in parentheses communicates a quiet and somewhat resigned cynicism. His is an anger cooling into submission. By this time, Abbot James, the superior at Gethsemani, had found out about Margie, partly due to Merton's own communicating to him about their phone calls. Merton thought it best to raise the topic with Dom James, since one of the brothers had already reported Merton for nighttime calls from the guest house. As might be expected, the abbot directed him to cut off all contact with her. Merton acknowledges regarding the "precise specifications" that "Maybe there is a kind of death in them, and maybe even a life comes out of them." He adds, "I don't question that there is probably something behind it all. I am still the guy who obeyed in *The Sign of Jonas*, and still riding in the whale's belly." (LTL, 305)

In other words, Merton is willing to admit that the rules of his monastic life hold values, not only objectively considered, but even personally; he has not, after all, abandoned being a monk.

Ending his relationship with Margie may be "a kind of death," but "maybe even a life comes out of them." However, this is small consolation in the present situation. Merton, of course, experienced and had written about what Jean-Francois Baudoz describes as the experience of the spiritual desert: "It is necessary to contemplate first—so that we may find the courage to face, in our turn, the struggle of the desert, that is, the struggle of life against death, of truth against lie, of reality against illusion." (Baudoz, 6) Merton holds out for a vestige of hope that even if he and Margie are no longer together, the thought of her would continue to feed his spirit:

No one can prevent us from thinking of each other and from loving each other. No one can change the fact that we belong to each other. That we have been through experiences of an incomparable love upon which no human being is entitled to pass the slightest judgment. No one can prevent me from remembering all these things. (LTL, 305)

At some moments in his journal and the *Midsummer Diary for M*, darkness far exceeds the light, and death dominates over any sense of life. Merton sees no way out of his dilemma except to attempt emotional detachment from Margie. While it feels like killing what he has come to believe is essential for growth, he cannot imagine any other solution. What looks to him like a hell on earth (and perhaps a hell in eternity should he judge and choose wrongly) results in a sort of paralysis. At least this is how it seems to be for him sometimes. Again, however, we hear an echo of hope that what looks like death may really not be. He writes this in the *Midsummer Diary for M*, allowing her to share in his thinking.

If God has brought her into my life and if God has willed our love, then it is more His affair than ours. My task consists in not forcing my love into a mold that pleases and reassures me (or both of us) but in leaving everything "open"—and not trying to predetermine the future. (LTL, 312)

Merton adds that he refuses "to believe that (God) is the kind of Joker that would want you to believe that the senseless makes sense." He reminds Margie that "This is a difficult business and it is the life of the desert, which is what I am involved in." He points out to her: "Because I am, you are too." (LTL, 307)

Merton realizes his struggle is not a solitary one, but it is all the more difficult because it creates a desert for her as well. It is on this point, more than any other, that we wish we could hear Margie's voice and thoughts. Surely she would have been as solicitous of Merton's feelings as he was of hers. But perhaps she also felt some of the resentment that many people have if they fall in love with someone who has already vowed to be faithful to another (whether that be in religious life or marriage) and knew that she could never compete with that vow, which had been freely given and intended for life. We, of course, will never know, which is what makes seeing their relationship only through the eyes and words of Merton so intriguing and yet so frustrating.

IX

Merton might have written:

Are we selfish?
I'm sure I am.
I don't like to accuse her
But isn't everyone in love?
For some time
I've known my empty place.
She's missed something, too,
In her short years.
And our two stunted selves
Expand and fill up with each other.
And it feels like nothing
We have ever known.
We want it. We both want the fullness
That satisfies our hungers
At least for moments.
Of course we're selfish.
We want each other
But we want this pleasure
Too
That tastes so good.

Merton did write:

May 24, 1966

Truth of the matter is that she needs me to need her. And that is exactly the last thing in the world I need: to be here in solitude with a 'need' for someone else!!" (LTL, 69)

. . . .

I now write:

Moments of objectivity and insight occur throughout Merton's journal and the *Midsummer Diary for M.* Woven among his proclamations of total and absolute love that holds no limitations, we see him step away, if only for a short time, and admit that everything is not perfect between them, which perfection is indeed basically impossible, as anyone who has loved another knows:

> *The thing is that we do not meet completely in our love: it is partial, not whole. There are aspects of ourselves, sides of ourselves that come together, are in harmony, respond deeply. But there are other sides which do not.* (LTL, 69)

New romance is always a time of nearly boundless delight. The whole world looks different in the glow of that kind of love. Merton tells us as much in page after page, with an intensity he had never experienced until this time. And we believe him if we have been there too.

He has periods of wisdom when he realizes that at fifty-one there is an embarrassing adolescence in what's happening to him. (It seems to be happening to Margie as well, although it is more appropriate to her in her twenties.) Despite his infatuation, Merton's years as a monk committed to spiritual reflection at the most profound level have taught him the ability to critique the situation. You can tell in his writings that because of such insights he has glimpsed what the differences in their ages and background and future desires would mean for anything permanent in his and Margie's relationship. He also knows his spiritual search for most of his life has involved deepening solitude, while her twenty-something enthusiasm is reaching for a growing sense of union with someone in intimate and exclusive love. And while these two realities can never be resolved, the pleasurable intensity of what they are experiencing together on all levels of intimacy leads Merton to ignore the inevitable consequences of their differences. Here in the *Midsummer Diary for M* he admits this thinking to her as he repeats what he had already written about in the pages of his journal a month before:

> *Have any two people ever sworn to each other such total and unending love? I guess all lovers do. But do we really mean it? Are we in a position to mean it? I think we are desperately trying to persuade ourselves and failing. Why do we think it necessary to persuade ourselves in the first place?* (LTL, 70)

Merton is aware that his desire for Margie has, in a way, distanced him from her. He talks about "the operations of love" and sees how these lead to the substitution of something he calls "love to the beloved herself." He continues, "For then love stands in the way between the lovers. It veils the goodness of the beloved. It dresses (or undresses) the beloved as a desirable object. Which is all right, too, except that one loves desire instead of the beloved." (LTL, 307)

What happens to this objectivity that Merton articulates so clearly for himself and for Margie throughout these months? One can only say that he allows himself to forget it in the very desires that he knows, when he is truthful, only make her less real to him. Why does he do this when at times he sees so clearly that the romance only distances them from each other? I would suggest he does so for the same reasons that anyone in the throes of romance does so. Merton is no different from anyone caught in the pleasures of early attraction and excitement. He is human, and he admits he is. However, the very admission of what he is doing testifies to an awareness few lovers have when it is happening to them. His fifty-one years of living and his time in the monastery have taught him some things; he is not entirely an adolescent in this relationship. But he is immature enough to go on doing what he knows makes no sense. He does so because, at least at times, he exhibits a conviction that continuing would teach him something he needed to learn.

These observations are not meant, in any way, to minimize what Merton and Margie had. It was clearly real. He (and I presume she) believed in it and acted upon it. But it was never going to "happen" the way they both wanted it to, because it couldn't. He was too old, too famous, too committed to the monastic life. She was perhaps too young, too outside of his world, too independent (we'll never really know her side of this story). The proof of all this surmise? Permanent commitment to each other never happened. Merton did not leave the monastery. They did not live "happily ever after." Margie went on to live her own life, which may well have included a husband and children.

The point is that these were two real human beings who loved each other but weren't able to be together. It happens. That doesn't mean that the rest of us can't learn from their experience.

X

Merton might have written:

Whatever led me
To buy a ticket for this ride?
Standing here waiting
It looked like fun.
Now,
Hanging on for dear life
I pray to get back to earth again.
As we climb to another height
I know there will be more to come
And I can't get off. I can only
Fall farther after every
Great upward sweep.
She clings to me
Tighter all the time,
This silly kid,
Because she thinks I'll protect her.
As if I could.

Merton did write:

June of 1966

The point is not to decide between this and that crazy answer when all the answers are crazy. There is no clear answer. Her fatal propensity is to need an answer. I can do without. Poor sweet kid, if only it were given me just to be the answer. But there is no answer, least of all me. I am nobody's answer, not even my own." (LTL, 308)

. . . .

I now write:

I can only wonder what it must have been like for Margie to read these words and hear herself called a "poor sweet kid." It seems that the reality of who Margie was—as well as who she was not—gradually began to dawn on Merton. (The same might well have been true of Margie regarding him.) While he had overlooked anything but what he saw as her perfection, both in herself and in her response to him, that phase in their relationship lasted a very short time. It ended with occasional flashes of awareness which he, early on, put aside to return to heights of ecstasy and impossible outcomes. He writes to himself and allows her to overhear in the *Midsummer Diary for M*: "All this torment comes from the contradictions I have allowed in myself by being open. By not closing all the gates and doors and carefully locking them and then winding myself in a blanket and going to sleep." (LTL, 309)

This sounds to me like the resignation to a still unhappy,

reluctantly considered option. It also sounds like Merton's bow to reality. At least part of that honest admission he shared with Margie. Perhaps he began to see how very young she really was. Maybe that was because of her response to him, her perceived (on his part) need for him. He had thought that he also had such a need for her, and he still did allow himself that thought at times. However, at other times he could not but realize that his life experience had provided much more practicality than she could be capable of at her age. His level of self-knowledge was beginning to reveal to him, if not to her, the complications that would grow over a prolonged relationship between them. His need for monastic solitude was something he could not for long deny. It was part of his very makeup as a person. However, early on he had sent her messages about his need for her, messages he had also sent to himself in his journal in the first days of their romance. Later, he backed off from such expressions of passion and inserted what he had come to see as objective facts about their relationship.

Merton eventually seemed to realize the degree to which he had encouraged Margie in this relationship, and at least at times forgave himself for what he admits was a daring relaxation of his usual reserve. He seemed to be reminding himself and her that "Necessarily, there are always new questions when you have not decided all the answers in advance." And he further excused himself for allowing himself to be vulnerable: "There is nothing *understandable* in love: just joy and then sorrow and then if you are lucky, more joy." (LTL, 309)

Their relationship apparently no longer seemed to him a stroke of luck, at least not entirely. Indeed, it appeared to be more of a roller coaster ride. His perception of Margie was that she was dealing with their love in a much less complicated way than he was. Perhaps he was trying to gently help her see what his greater age, self-perceived honesty, and assumed wisdom had begun to reveal to him. In the *Midsummer Diary for M* he makes an effort to reveal to her what he had come to understand—in the presumed hope that she would also be able to receive and embrace that same understanding.

The man who could write with such eloquent clarity about the deceptions of the false self and the freedom of the true, could not help but look at himself in relation to Margie with the same sharp lens. At least sometimes this was the case. And when he did so, there was no escaping again—at least not for long—into the realm of romance. Merton's definition of love was moving, at least sometimes, beyond the ecstasy to something deeper and, even if less exciting, more truthful. He seemed to be gently trying to let Margie know of his love for her, which was undeniable, and yet tell her what sacrifices it would demand of him.

Many people might call this effort a testimony to his profound spirituality, the gift he has communicated to so many people so articulately in his writings. Merton remained only a short time in the wild world of love based on touch and sexual excitement. As comforting and satisfying as this message was to him, it soon gave way to more practical and concrete admissions. He began again to approach the present from his more contemplative stance of humility, the monastic virtue at the heart of the *Rule of Benedict* that was so much a part of his history—of his very Cistercian being. This virtue, sometimes described as a straightforward acknowledgment of what is so and embracing it, soon led him to see deeper into his own need, a need that no human being could satisfy, not even the warm, caring Margie:

> Everybody else says 'turn back,' as if there were some norm in the past that I had to recover. That is what is impossible, there is no "back to normal." The normal is now, on the way

to the unthinkable. To what I cannot know because it has
not even begun to develop. I beg God that it may develop
in us both together and that we may somehow share it, and
that it will be only one thing: love. (LTL, 339)

In the end, Merton realized that this is the only kind of love possible between them. His hope is that Margie, too, will be willing to see and accept it.

XI

Merton might have written:

She wants a husband
And some kids.
I want my hermitage
In the woods.
And this means
we aren't possible.
I've tried to make myself clear
But she doesn't believe me.
And maybe I don't either.
Maybe she hears
Something deeper in my whole being
Than my thoughts grasp
Or my words say.
Problem is:
I don't know
Which one of us
Is really listening.

Merton did write:

June of 1966

...I think too much, and try to decide too much, because I think there are so many things I have to decide. And in a way there are. I am bound to decisions and that is the trouble. But the whole life I am living is a life filled with total uncertainty and I have to be constantly re-deciding, because I refuse the fake certainty of conforming and allowing everything to be decided beforehand by others." (LTL, 308)

. . . .

I now write:

One of Merton's great gifts was his refusal to live on the surface. Because of this gift he plumbed the depths of himself and the circumstances of his life, both interior and in relationship with others. Also because of this gift, he uncovered the deceptions of the false self and the freedom and rightness of the true. Of all his contributions to the spirituality of the twentieth century, perhaps the greatest was his laying bare for us to see how we lie to ourselves in order to defend ourselves against our own perceived annihilation. He named and described the dynamic of the human ego creating lies to ourselves as a defense and was able to articulate for others the depth of humility called for on the spiritual journey. Only when fear and falsehood are overcome can we see and embrace the limited creatures we are and become serious about the pursuit of truth and the reality of

God's mercy and love.

Such gifts as Merton possessed, however, can also be our downfall, and I believe they often are when we exaggerate them into compulsion. This journal of Merton's crisis of relationship with Margie seems to me to witness to this dynamic. He could write and speak as arguably no other person of his time was able to do about the necessity to look deeply into one's actions and motives. And yet, his very exploration became, at least for a time, an obsession where Margie was concerned. I know of no other way to describe what is written in this journal as he agonized about how to get to the heart of the matter. He did so with a ruthlessness he probably hoped would end his internal struggles and bring him to a peaceful resolution of some kind, but it never did. Merton, in fact, did not handle this matter very well. How could he? He was human.

There is a Norwegian folk tale that captures this dynamic of Merton's for me. In it, a man named Peer Gynt peels an onion, layer by layer, searching for the core. What he discovers is that there is no core; the onion consists only of many layers. The journal of this time in Merton's life seems to be only one example of his tendency to over-analyze, to pull off and set aside every possible aspect of a problem. To do so, however, led him not to insight and awareness but only along many pathways that ended up nowhere and with nothing. This is why, I think, reading his journal from the time can become confusing and frustratingly repetitive for the reader. Where is Merton, and what is it he really wants or believes in? These questions could be answered more than one way, depending on the date of the journal entry.

The value of this obsessive personality trait in Merton is that he explored for all of us every possible way we may think of to hide from our reality. He himself often spoke of the need to question, even when no answers were forthcoming. The very questioning, turning around and examining something from all angles, only ended for him with an awareness of the fruitlessness of such a pursuit. Seeing this fruitlessness, he was eventually forced to wait for and to allow the truth to emerge. The hundreds of pages in this volume of his journal represent Merton's search for solution and culminate in the futility of finding that solution in himself. Pride has many faces, and it seems to me that this journal exposes the features of one of those faces Merton knew well. As a result, he ultimately discovered not knowledge that settled the whole scene for him but the wisdom of allowing answers to surface out of a humble acceptance of what "was so."

> I see clearly that we are both torn by contradictions. She cannot go on indefinitely without full sexual expression of our love, though she thinks she can (and fears she cannot. We discussed this frankly.) She knows she is attracted to others and to opportunities of passion in spite of love for me and I know I have no right to hold her and do not want to: in the sense that I think she ought to marry. (LTL, 79)

Merton wrote these words in his journal in early June of 1966, but they do not constitute an end to his efforts around finding a way to make his relationship with Margie a possible, if limited, part of their lives together. He went through some more rounds of doubting what he foresaw must happen down the line: a complete breaking off of contact with Margie. Rationalization kept creeping back, often for both of them. No matter how many layers of possibilities they considered, each layer continued to be abandoned as impossible. Even though the mist seemed to clear and reveal the concrete reality, at least to him, that their relationship must eventually end, it would cloud over again out of his desire to salvage something of what they had known together:

"I see that I have to really *love her* and not just love love or love her body. It is a training in realism and in love of *the person* she is (a person inexhaustibly beautiful and lovable to me)." (LTL, 80)

Merton searched desperately for the kind of love that he realized, at least sometimes in his journal, would be all he would ever be able to offer Margie. Still, he kept returning to the question of whether he was deceiving himself or not. Did Margie really have the intuition that it was right for him to put their relationship ahead of his monastic commitment? Did she know better than he that he needed to respond to a new vocational call, one that was the true path to a wholeness he could never find as a monk? These were the questions he believed he had to consider.

Sometimes his answer to all these questions was a clear no: "...my vocation is not a formality that I can evade or set aside with a mental operation. On the contrary, it is built more deeply into my experience than anything else in the world, and I am now completely identified with it." This he wrote later on in June in his *Midsummer Diary for M.* And he goes on to add, "Yet secretly I am glad that she thinks there is something else in me besides the monk and the priest, although she knows I am a priest perhaps better than I do." (LTL, 331)

As monk, priest, and lover, Merton peels off his analyses one by one, but still, at some points in this process, he cannot or will not accept himself as essentially monk/priest, even while still at times proclaiming this priority as his true identity. Even Margie accepts him as monk/priest, though she seems to maintain that the identity of "lover" does and needs to continue to be Merton's primary reality. Her frank assessment of this at least leads him to continue to consider for a time that she might well be right in her assumption. It also allows him to keep away from the core of a conclusion and instead perpetuate his peeling the onion of layers of analysis. If there is any false self here, it would seem to be that in order to avoid inevitable truth about their relationship Merton continues to keep alive the questioning and not admit he knows the final answer. Reality and truth would end his obsessions and finally result in a peace beyond his mental machinations, but throughout this time he tells himself he must not lie to himself—and fears that to dismiss her assessment of their future might be to do just that. Therefore, his warning to himself against falsehood, which is itself a falsehood, keeps him in a characteristic frenzy of activity and reflection that fills this volume of journal entries:

> *The problems of love arise out of a certain mythology about love: the "they lived happily ever after" myth, or the more modern one of sexual fulfillment, etc. We can't help thinking in those terms, we are conditioned that way. In my own life such thinking is supremely misleading, because I have chosen a different way, a different dimension. You can't judge by five standards at once. (LTL, 337)*

At another level, Merton tells himself that he might be wrong and Margie might be right. This lie allows him to put off seeing the truth, which he sometimes hopes might really be falsehood. So onward he goes, telling himself "...and what I really have to do is the same thing I have always had to do: to find my own way, without a map, taking neither this nor that except in so far as I have to, and working it out as I go along." (LTL, 338)

And so the cycles of clarity and questioning in Merton revolve again and again. It is interesting that they do so from the very gift he has shared with so many others, an awareness of how we deceive ourselves. No wonder he could write so eloquently on that subject. He came to know at fifty-one, and had indeed known earlier on in his life, that falsehood can wear many faces. Sometimes it even masquerades as radical authenticity.

XII

Merton might have written:

I'm found out.
Now what?
It's not just the two of us anymore
Or the friends I've found I can talk to.
It's the Powers that Be
Here,
The ones who know me
Less and less
All the time.
But maybe I'm wrong;
Maybe they are smarter
Than I think.
At least I might have some sense
If I can say that much.
There are others, too,
Who see things their way
And others who just keep
Their mouths shut
And say nothing at all.
Whoever anybody is
Makes no difference.
What is it that I say?
That's what counts
More than the whole Greek Chorus
With its words and silences;
More even than her
Single, sweet voice.

Merton did write:

June 12, 1966

...I certainly realize the real spiritual danger I have got into. Things have really got close to going wrong and it is providential that everything has been blocked at the moment. Perhaps it is saving me from a real wreck. Jim Wygal on the phone Saturday was saying 'Be careful you don't destroy yourself!' He is perhaps more right than I thought at the time." (LTL, 82)

. . . .

I now write:

The third of the monastic vows which the *Rule of Benedict* speaks about is obedience. Cistercians base their monasticism on this fifth century document and the spiritual path it outlines for the monks who choose to follow it. The abbot is believed to hold the place of Christ in the monastery, and ultimate decisions are his, despite the fact that the *Rule of Benedict* also requires consultation with the monastic community for important decision-making. (Such a collegial, collaborative prescription was an innovation in that period of time of Benedict.) Modern monastic communities usually keep the original spirit of involving community members in decision-making in their contemporary adaptations. The primacy of the abbot's role, however, has remained over the centuries, as it surely did at Gethsemani Abbey during Merton's time. We see him cognizant of and respectful toward the role of the abbot in monastic life.

However, Merton's ability to assess personality at a deeper level was also one of his gifts, as we find in many of his journal and letter-writing comments.

Much has been written by Merton and others about his difficulties with a series of abbots during his lifetime. Merton's personal story and temperament, his emphasis on what was life-giving rather than on rules and regulations of the law, his attraction to the hermit life with its opportunity for individual day-to-day decision-making, surely played into some of the tensions between him and his superiors. Merton was also often an astute judge of character and he found, at least at this point in his life, that Abbot James was not only insensitive to his situation and that of others in the community but a superficial administrator. This description was clearly not meant as a compliment, but as a statement of lack of spiritual leadership, something so important to Merton's spirituality:

> *I ought to have more compassion for the Abbot.... But his judgments of others are made in relation to his own power hunger—and how they affect his security. He is really a tragic person and has no idea of it. And the monastery will have to feel the effects, and indeed does. (LTL, 169)*

His journal contains many commentaries on Dom James' personality and relationship with community members and with Merton. The themes Merton discusses concerning the Abbot's general personality traits become at this time in his life particularized around the relationship with Margie. To his credit, Abbot James acts appropriately for a religious superior of his time regarding how to deal with "a monk in love with a woman" (LTL, 84) as Merton put it when he and Margie were finally discovered. Merton, having assessed the abbot already as being superficial, was certain that Dom James could not understand the significance and depth of what was going on between Margie and him. The abbot's decision to order Merton to break off all ties with Margie immediately was inconceivably wrong for Merton; in his eyes it would be an unloving act for him to do so. In the early pages of his *Midsummer Diary for M*, he comments about a meeting with Dom James:

> *The Abbot did (joyfully) all the negating he thought he had to do. All the joyful depriving, all the assurances that he knows what I suffer. What I suffer?... What do they think about her suffering? It does not enter their heads. Hence I cannot take seriously what they pretend to say about my suffering. It is just they themselves are anxious. (LTL, 304)*

The Abbot's insensitivity seems all the more poignant when Merton thinks of it as manifested toward Margie. Yet the fact remains that the Abbot was the one Merton had accepted as the person who takes the place of Christ in the monastery. At the same time, however, Merton sees Abbot James as not fulfilling the compassionate role that the *Rule of Benedict* demands of him. There exists, besides the abbot's power and responsibility, a necessity in Merton's eyes that the abbot keep before him the predominance of love. To obey the abbot on this issue seems to Merton to be "absurd." He could bow to it only with an honesty that proclaims he does not agree with it. When he does obey in that way, he is able to "express the absurd and at the same time to reject it, to be free from it." This solution, he says, is the only way to obtain "complete freedom from the absurdity that is imposed by *every* form of institutional life." He goes on to say that life outside the monastery would be "to succumb to the greater absurdity." (LTL, 306)

We can only wonder what Margie made of such a convoluted moral solution and whether Merton ever thought she could understand what he was talking about. He was acutely aware that she had nobody to talk to, while at the same time admitting that neither did he; nobody among "confessors and all the other boy scouts available on the premises" (LTL, 308) understood what he and she were experiencing.

There were others who tried to tell Merton he was on a path that he should not follow. (Jim Wygal, his therapist and friend, expressed clearly what he thought, as at least the June 12 entry attests.) When Merton talks about the objections people have about the relationship, he often uses the pronoun "they," without usually identifying who "they" are. Against that group, he feels solitary and is reminded of the reality that he alone is experiencing this love with Margie—from the confusing aspect of his personal responsibility to his vow of obedience and his very real love for her.

Something of what faith means to him comes into play here. Thomas Merton must approach any decision not from knowledge or stoicism, he insists, but only from the virtue of faith. Somehow for him, "Faith and revolt are inseparable. Faith is the fundamental revolt." (LTL, 312)

Whatever is going on in Merton and Margie's relationship, it was clear to him that they were meant to meet and to deal with the consequences of that meeting: "If God has brought her into my life and if God has willed our love, then it is more His affair than ours." (LTL, 312)

Once again, the depths of Merton's intellectual analysis provide no answers. He returns to the point, saying, "My task consists in not forcing my love into a mold that pleases and reassures me (or both of us), but in leaving everything 'open'—and not trying to predetermine the future." (LTL, 312)

What does love demand? What does obedience demand? He chooses to wait and see once again because no direction seems clear to him.

Is it clear to us much of the time?

XIII

Merton might have written:

God,
I need your mercy
More than anything else.
I'm trying to be honest,
But I know myself
And this other need I have
Of her.
Something tells me I'm telling the truth
To me.
Something wonders if it's all the truth
Or if I've buried a piece of it
From both of you.
I long for
And I need
Your comfort and hers,
Or maybe I did and now
I only need yours,
Coming cloaked in a strength
I hate to admit.
What I really need is the whole Truth
And that is you.
But most of all I need your mercy
For those lies
Deeper than anything else.

Merton did write:

July 31, 1966

Suddenly I find myself looking from the outside into a world of religious correctness which has to some extent become alien. And that is the whole trouble. It is also the source of confusion.

"You are no longer correct, as you used to be." For twenty-five years I have been an edification but now.... Yet strangely now I feel real, though wrong. The correctness leaves me terribly uneasy!" (LTL, 105)

. . . .

I now write:

Despite the many absolute, definitive assertions Merton made in his journal (and he certainly made enough of them), perhaps the most operative word for his enduring state of mind at this period in his life is the word "confused." This confusion came back again and again to Margie and his need to discern that what he experienced with her was real, even though it was somehow wrong. Keeping the rules, being correct, being edifying—these are things that led Merton to an uneasiness... and such uneasiness is an important thing for all of us to consider in any attempt at real discernment.

Sometimes, however, Merton's assessments do appear clear to him: "I know I have been naïve and imprudent." (LTL, 105)

But no matter what his intense personal reflections on his relationship with Margie, there seems to be no limit to his need to analyze them.

Another significant feeling Merton has is that the deceptive behaviors around his communications with Margie have also left him feeling unsettled. He comments, "I am really relieved at not having to continue that complex double game of letters, phone calls, etc. (No trouble admitting this was all wrong. Not just a matter of external correctness but of inner unity and consistency.)" (LTL, 105)

Here is another important clue about what might be the truth beneath much of the confusion he has written about. He has felt dishonest, not only with Margie but with everyone around him.

By July of 1966, Merton is acknowledging the distinction between correctness and authenticity. There is much more depth to him than simply to put aside as superficial and legalistic the monastery's rules as they are laid out. He sees that he is overlooking his interior dishonesty by childishly sneaking around them. He asserts again and again that his love for Margie is undeniable; it seems to be that the way he is dealing with it is what is causing him unrest. Yet on July 27 he says clearly that "...the whole thing is obviously over, as far as the meetings and lovemaking are concerned and we both know it and have 'accepted it' I imagine," and he then adds, "but as for my love—of this there is no question, in it there is no change." (LTL, 101-102)

What is it that causes him to still feel confused about how he needs to act? Perhaps the answer to that question is what he had written earlier on June 10: "Her love is not just 'another question' and 'another problem'—it is right at the center of all my questions and problems and right at the center of my hermit life." (LTL, 81)

It cannot be denied that Merton always seemed willing to take time to be thorough in his internal spiritual searching, which is no doubt one of the reasons he cannot simply cut off all relationship with Margie as he was told to do. He had freely chosen to risk walking into the questions raised by their relationship, and so he accepted responsibility to consider them carefully because of their essential place in determining the larger truth about who he was. In the *Midsummer Diary for M*, written in June, Merton says:

> *Since the thing that is most important to me is the deepening and the exploration of consciousness, then obviously if I catch myself lying about that I will be deeply embarrassed. Perhaps that was part of the bump too. Pretending that sitting here drinking beer was actually a sort of enrichment of an unhappy solitude. Nuts. (LTL, 344)*

I continue to wonder what Margie was possibly making of his tortured struggles, some of which might have had parallels in her own life. Some of Merton's concerns, however, were distinctly monastic, and they created at least a layer of concern that she could not have had. He tells her, "And now for my own part, I do have to get down to my job of solitude. Though when you look at it too close it gets confusing, and there are no real blueprints for it." (LTL, 347)

Here is that word "confusing" again. He is aware that what is going on within him is something Margie simply cannot know how to help him with: "Who knows what it means to be so utterly alone before God with decisions and choices that no one else agrees with or approves of, yet which conscience dictates. That is a much more frightening desert than one of rocks and sand where one is living an 'approved' monastic life." (LTL, 347)

Perhaps Merton realizes that no matter how much she loves him, Margie is unable to comprehend what he is talking about in these issues around living monastic life. We'll never know what she thought or was capable of understanding. The point is that we always have only his side of the story: "But there is no use my talking about it. Even you do not agree with me on this, I guess." (LTL, 347)

I wonder to this day if Merton decided that Margie could not accept what he was saying about monastic life or whether the reality was that he felt she could not even comprehend it. The first case would have shown a doubt about her compassion and empathy for him; the second would have shown a doubt about her knowledge of and insight into him.

Merton clearly sees himself alone in this struggle, which is odd for someone who professes to be head-over-heals in love with another person. He had written in the past that only God can be with someone in a place where there is no path. That may seem an unusual statement for a person who values religious community, and I'm sure it sounds unusual to a happily married couple. But not only had Merton learned to turn to that God over the years, not only had he encouraged others to do so in his writings—in his relationship with Margie he seems to have come again to the realization that there is no other sanctuary for him than one-on-one with the divine. This belief goes deeper into his life now than perhaps at any time before.

While he is certain of his love for Margie, he realizes that he has not handled it well from the start. In April of 1966 he admits: "In my heart I knew it would really have been better if I had followed my original intuition and been content with a couple of letters and nothing more." (LTL, 44)

And yet, think of what Merton would have missed had he followed his instinct then! He somehow never regretted his relationship with Margie, flawed as it may have been. But the results of that risk they both took turned out to be not only confusing to Merton (and presumably to Margie) but messy as well. A merciful God would have to forgive both of them for the mess.

XIV

Merton might have written:

*If there ever was a shy word,
It's "love,"
One that hides what it is from everybody
Or at least from me.
When I see her
I ache until and while
We touch.
And is that "love"?
I hear her saying she wants me
Not only now, but always.
"Always" I don't hear
Because "now" is so loud
It drowns "always" out.
Should I pay better attention
I ask sometimes,
And is that "love"?
I know, when I'm honest,
That my "always," what I call "love,"
Is different from hers.
Knowing that, am I faced with
Something else
Also called "love"?*

Merton did write:

June of 1966

She asks of my solitude that it have in it a place for her in which she is always known, reverenced, loved, valued, prized for herself as she is in her actuality. I will never refuse her this: it is the root of my commitment and my fidelity to give her this anchor in my own sea of loneliness. Forever. (LTL, 311)

. . . .

I now write:

There is no question Merton believed he would carry his love for Margie into the future, wherever his life took him. We must give him that. The fact is he only had to keep that promise for two years, at least in this world, something he could not have foreseen, even though it has been intimated by some of his friends that he had some premonition of an early death.

In his *Midsummer Diary for M*, given to her in June of 1966, Merton has no trouble promising this to Margie. Despite his realization that they will never live together—never even live in close proximity as friends—he wants her to know how significant she is to him. He does so in this series of verbs that surround her being with a regard and respect that he promises will never end.

There are those who think Merton used Margie in a selfish and lustful way, merely satisfying his physical needs and mining the psychological and spiritual insights he gained from the relationship. Some wonder to this day, more than fifty years later, whether he was ever really concerned for her welfare or only for his personal spiritual growth, pursued throughout his journal's sometimes savage internal searching.

As an unofficial commentator on their relationship, with only his words and my understanding of his personality to lean on, it seems to me that Merton did feel compelled to understand exactly the nature for him of their relationship and the place she had come to hold in his life's story. But there are too many passages of beautiful concern for her and compassion for her suffering for his self-absorption to be the whole truth. There was a profound, contemplative dimension to her presence for him that he assures her of: "To be alone in a solitude that is with you, though without your bodily presence, is certainly a special kind of freedom: as though we were even free of time and space, and could be together at will in our love, in all its simplicity." (LTL, 319)

Thomas Merton accuses himself of causing her suffering. He should have realized early on that he could never be the person she was looking for. In his denial of that fact, he led her to believe they could possibly be partners for a lifetime:

> I have not been either a good monk or a good lover. I have been nothing. I have tried to be things that were incompatible and have ended up only hurting her and leaving her sorrowful, confused, pained. In getting the pieces of my own life together I have really done little that can help her: except I honestly feel that in being myself I can help her best. (LTL, 334)

It took Merton a very short time, probably not more than a

month, to acknowledge the unreality of the relationship he had clearly encouraged—first in himself and then in Margie—in the early days of their tumbling into romance. However, neither could he ever deny his honest commitment to her person. To honor this commitment, he would have to share with her the truth that they could never live the life they had fantasized about.

"All this shows, once again, that you cannot love without getting hurt," Merton admits to her. He goes on to say, "In the first place it does not worry me that I am hurt, but that I may be hurting her." He takes the blame for what developed, but not all of it: "...We both know enough to anticipate that we would be badly mangled in this inevitable separation and we went toward it with our eyes open." (LTL, 334)

Merton does assume what he sees as his total responsibility for their pain, and he does so only a few sentences after refusing to shoulder it entirely: "But the trouble is that I am weak and insecure and let myself get shaken: and then let her see that I am shaken, and this may perhaps unnerve her and make her start blaming herself—as if there were anything to blame herself for." (LTL, 335)

Again, we can only wonder what Margie might have heard in these back and forth analyses where she is referred to in the third person. Merton seems to wonder the same thing when he turns from his self-preoccupation and addresses her directly: "Poor darling, don't let me hurt you by my stupidity and uncertainty. I do love you and will never stop loving you, and I believe in your love, too." (LTL, 335)

Ten years earlier, the psychiatrist Gregory Zilboorg had called Merton a narcissist to his face. If Zilboorg read the journal of 1966, he might have been confirmed in his analysis. But perhaps instead we see here a personality trait that propelled Merton throughout his life to pursue all of his experiences to their radical depth; he insisted on stripping himself of all false-hood. In this relationship with Margie, he is driven to be honest with himself as never before because of the significance of her in-fluence on him and the basic questions about his life choices that their relationship presented. Consumed with the mental efforts of this dynamic, however, Merton does seem at times to forget the living individual who is the center of his concern.

Yet if Merton ever overcame his tendency to overly-intellec-tualize and so distance himself from the living persons he was musing about, it seems to have been with Margie. He keeps re-turning to a genuine compassion that testifies to her living pres-ence for him.

Merton seems to have been born with the life view in which bodily experiences become essential symbols for spiritual growth. For the first time in their relationship, he discovered the necessi-ty to act out physically what he had theoretically discovered and written about: the message of love in all of its dimensions and the truth it teaches to those who give and those who receive it. It is small wonder that he spent seemingly endless rounds conclud-ing, abandoning the conclusions, and eventually bowing to the mystery of what he could only call "love."

Did he abandon Margie in this process? Did she become only a symbolic means for his internalizing the essential learn-ing so long overdue? Some people answer "yes" to that question, but I believe there is adequate information to join those who answer "no." Margie became and remained for Merton a concrete individual whom he loved and who loved him. It seems to me he spoke this truthfully and lovingly when he told her, "I want only your happiness, and if that happiness means marrying and lov-ing another, it is just what I want for you." (LTL, 346)

XV

I walk my woods
In the dark
With silence all around,
Except maybe the rustling
Of some small creature
I've disturbed is there.
Or maybe it's my footsteps
In dry leaves.
But that's all the sound
Around me.
Inside me there's what I can only call
Shouting—or maybe
Longing screams.
It's hard to tell.
The dark is
Outside and within.
I know these woods
And move with confidence
Out here;
But inside me there's only
Jumbled noise
That adds up to nothing much.
My Love feels close at times,
And I feel all terribly alone
At others.
In my silent place
That shrieks at me.

Merton did write:

July 29, 1966

Was so torn by loneliness and longing to talk with her—and knowing it was hopeless. Worse still driving out on the turnpike—first passing near the hospital. I thought I was slowly being torn in half. Then several times while I was reciting the office deep silent cries came slowly tearing and rending their way up out of the very ground of my being.... There was nothing I could do with these metaphysical howls. Getting back to the hermitage finally calmed them. (LTL, 104)

. . . .

I now write:

Thomas Merton was nothing if not dramatic. After all, he was a poet. So many of his journal entries tell of the anguish he experienced through this entire period of his life. It is probably true that he had met many other moments in his past with this characteristic passionate abandon. Nevertheless, it is no wonder that he recognized unusual intensity in this watershed relationship with Margie; it had changed his entire view of his personal goodness and worth and opened the floodgates of his emotion, sensuality, and sexuality. He was seeing himself in the depths of his human vulnerability as never before. And he was also admitting that this new person he had become because of Margie could create a similar response in her.

In the July 29 entry of his journal above he describes his restlessness and pain. He is thinking of those who consider what is happening between him and Margie as unlawful, and he calls their world "stupid, trite, artificial." (LTL, 104)

He does acknowledge the wisdom of those with moral standards that outlaw the "imperative reality" of their love. They are the practical ones who do not know the anguish he is in over what is to him something he cannot control any more than he could control his breathing or heartbeat. On the one hand, these people make sense: "I know that if we really let go I would be destroyed and so would she. And yet—would it not be worth it after all? I know she thinks so—tonight I wonder about it again." (LTL,104)

Pain can cause even the reasoned conclusion he spoke about in the *Midsummer Diary for M* to be looked at once again. He quickly adds, however, in the very next sentence: "But I know I have something else to do. The rain and the frogs are saying it clearly enough." He cannot deny the other truth that the concrete surroundings of his hermitage remind him of. (LTL, 104)

Back in June he had written to Margie: "I am of no value to you except in so far as I am this absurd man all alone on a wooded hill, with the darkness falling all around him, the stars coming out over his head." (LTL, 315)

Merton now views himself as being immersed in difficult and alienating interpersonal relationships with others that have been caused by their love. His spiritual life has been affected, because he is now, "a man who has no clear ideas about God but just hangs around waiting to be struck by God as if by lightning...." (LTL, 315)

This is a powerful image of God, and he points out to Margie, in contrast, what a weak human being he is: "That is what you have chosen to love, my darling, and that is the strange being who will love you forever, even when the lightning strikes...." (LTL, 315)

85

On more than one occasion, Merton lets his readers look behind the door of his hermitage to know the thoughts about Margie that haunt him there despite his efforts to put them out of his mind. He also entertains fantasies about her when he cannot sleep:

> *Obsessed with the idea that M might conceivably find her way out here though she has never seen the place and could not possibly find it in the dark, etc. If only there were a soft knock on the door, and I opened it, and it was she standing on the porch. Finally I couldn't stand it anymore and got up, put my clothes on and started wandering around.* (LTL, 315-316)

He feels "a complete prisoner under these stars. With nothing. Or perhaps everything."(LTL, 316)

Sitting on his famous porch that night, his rationalizations stop and he sits there in emptiness, knowing somehow that what is nothing and empty holds all that is. His knowledge of Zen and his life of Christian contemplation have taught him that much. He cannot race anywhere in his mind any longer, and so he is simply there, present with "Fireflies, stars, darkness, the massive shadows of the woods, the vague dark valley. And nothing, nothing, nothing." He thinks about writing a poem, but gives that up because you "don't write poems about nothing." (LTL, 316)

Then things take another turn, or perhaps open up to another realization and its consequent interior quiet: "I look at the south sky and for some ungodly reason for which there is no reason, everything is complete. I think of going back to bed, in peace without knowing why, a peace that cannot be justified by anything, any reason, any proof, any argument. Any supposition." The concreteness of the hermitage and its surroundings bring him out of his head and into his body once again. "There are no suppositions left. Only fireflies." (LTL, 316)

Nature has done its work on him once more. The Abbot had thought it was not good for Merton to be alone in his hermitage and told him so. Instinctively, Merton seemed to know otherwise and had resisted any suggestion that he come back to live in the community. That instinct proved correct, it seems to me. Once again, perhaps some of Merton's best poetry—although he would probably not even recognize it as poetry—was written in his confrontation with both inanimate and sentient creation around him. Also, his deepest answer to all the questioning of this time in his relationship with his beloved Margie is discovered in this place when his thinking fails him and he is brought to a shared quiet with his surroundings. He tells her this in his own words in the *Midsummer Diary for M*:

> *I cannot have enough of the hours of silence when nothing happens. When the clouds go by. When the trees say nothing. When the birds sing.... It would be so much more wonderful to be all tied up in someone, to work for someone, to come home and love her, to have a child; and I know inexorably that this is not for me.* (LTL, 341)

There are probably those who, when reading this passage, are saddened by the words, as Merton seemed at least somewhat to be. But I see here his strong realization that his life of solitude is an innate priority and a clear vocation. Like so many others, and perhaps all of us, "what ifs" can be entertained. They do not, however, cancel out the ground of our love and our truth. One wonders whether Margie could hear his sure voice and accept it, at least by summer of 1966. It must have been incredibly hard to do so on her part. After all, this certitude of Merton's about his monastic vocation so frequently alternated with questioning it and with disappointment at his specific living situation. I wonder when she stopped hoping that they could make a life together, when she discovered the inevitable about their relationship that he was so reluctant at times to admit to himself…and to her.

XVI

Merton might have written:

I know
This has to end.
Everything in me
And outside me
Tells me so.
I'm convinced.
But wait awhile.
Not quite yet.
Hang on—
Onto her and our times
Together.
When you pull off a bandaid
You can choose
The firm shock of all at once
Or else do it slowly
With the pain spread longer.
And this hurts more,
Maybe.
But it is what I choose.

Merton did write:

June 23, 1966

(I do not deny there is a certain logic in separating us, but why can't we sometimes write to each other, or talk to each other on the phone? If things were not so unreasonable here, we would have gone less far, for we would have been visiting nicely like everyone else within view of the gatehouse and talking properly like good children. It could have gone on a long time and no damage to anyone.) (LTL, 336)

. . . .

I now write:

I wonder if it is really true that the rules and restrictions of the monastery were what led Merton and Margie to keep their relationship hidden. Apparently, at least at times, Merton thought they were, as this passage above from the diary he sent to Margie says, albeit with a cynical twist. However, I also wonder whether he was being realistic, considering how quickly they both knew that their relationship was not platonic but that romance and sexuality had been part of things from the beginning. Merton's suspicion that his love for Margie was something he had never before experienced—and that it might get out of hand—was evident at least from Margie's first letter to him, and perhaps earlier from their introduction when he was her patient. That awareness, initially subtle and unspoken, turned out to be well founded. Perhaps the intensity might have been delayed somewhat by circumstances that fit Gethsemani's regulations for visitors, but it seems likely that it eventually would have accelerated to a point where they would want and be led to have more intimate meetings.

Merton's cynicism stated, often clearly, that he felt Dom James and the others who knew about their relationship were dismissing the depth of the love between Margie and him. At least Merton, if not Margie, felt demeaned and dismissed by the implication that what they were experiencing was not much more than a delayed adolescent fling: "No one can say that our love has nothing to do with the truth of our lives—as if it were something like an attack of the flu or an unfortunate accident. That is the logic behind the prohibitions that have been inflicted on me." (LTL, 336)

Merton wanted to honor their love, and he insisted to himself and to Margie that he valued its depth. It was not something for him that could be simply cut off without respectful gentleness and great anguish.

Despite his reverence for this part of his journey and hers, however, he admitted that he has not handled it well from early on: "It is of course easy enough to look back and say that 'here' or 'there' I should have turned another corner and got off the road." But he added, "... it was not possible to get off that road. I was on it before I knew it, and going fast." He accepted the responsibility of what had increased the momentum between them and acknowledged that "At one point she saw the danger far more clearly than I did—and I talked her out of it. Or rather she saw how good my intentions were, and the basic innocence of it...." (LTL, 326)

So Margie, some twenty-five years younger than he, seemed to him to have been less naïve. She saw sooner than he did the impossibility of the kind of relationship they both initially were hoping to have. Merton was genuinely concerned for her, and wondered how she was accepting the idea that they had to end what had been so significant for both of them:

> *The most intolerable thing of all is not to know what she feels, whether or not she needs my help, whether or not I can do something for her. Perhaps after all the most helpful thing is that we are kept apart in spite of ourselves.* (LTL, 326)

In many places and times, Merton affirms the beauty and integrity of the bond between them, something he was convinced of and which few, if any besides the two of them, seemed able to understand. He was not sure how she could accept the fact that they cannot go on seeing one another and how the ending of everything they have known, short-lived as it was, would affect her:

> *I felt that if we had only had a chance, we could have grown magnificently together into a beautiful dual organism of love: we could have slowly healed and strengthened each other, brought out all that was waiting to develop, that was blocked, that was held back by society... Dear, we must not forget the reality of our love and the reality of the sharing, the penetration of our mutual secrets. We have really done this and done it much more than lovers ordinarily do."* (LTL, 326-327)

During August of 1966, Merton's thoughts are turning to community issues: Dom James and his leadership, the institutional limitations of Gethsemani's life, the lack of spiritual stimulation in the monastery, the inability of community life to bring a monk to full maturity. He has not contacted Margie for a month, nor does he plan to do so (see LTL, 270-289).

Late in July he had written that he had no real desire to get in touch with her. His work load is taking his attention, and he hopes to spend more time on his spiritual life: "I know that what I have to do is work on my meditation, and on the kind of life that people forget exists. And she is no help in that." There is resignation in his words, but he adds: "Yet I felt so much more real when we were in love. And yet too I know how much illusion was in it. (Or at least I can make a good guess!)" (LTL, 269)

Time and time again, Merton tells himself that their love has been real, if imperfect. Whenever he writes about this in the journal, he accuses himself of personal deception. However, he is quick to add that the lie around their relationship which he could not let go of for some weeks was precisely what brought him in touch with his vulnerability. Had he been strong and disciplined with Margie from the beginning, he would not have learned the difference between romance and real love, nor would he ever have seen and embraced his own flawed humanity so profoundly. Many of his journal entries at this time return to these thoughts. They interweave a real concern for Margie with a refusal to simply walk away from her. Toward the end of August, he acknowledges that maybe a definite break with Margie would be the merciful thing, but he refuses to "say anything that sounds like 'I do not want to see you or hear from you again.'" (LTL, 118)

Not only would that be inconceivable to him; it would be a different kind of lie, although both of them seem to know clearly that their times together are over.

Real love always means suffering, Merton reminds himself. He acknowledges that in some ways she might be in greater pain than he is, and he writes: "I don't know what to do except to go on loving and occasionally slipping a letter out to her somehow. This I think I owe her besides needing it myself." (LTL, 119)

Later he adds: "I think a love like ours demands some human concession." (LTL, 119-120)

Finally, Merton accepts the responsibility for the decision to lessen their contact gradually. He hopes to avoid hurting both of them more than necessary. Everyone, he says, thinks it would be best—and easier—just to break it all off at once. But for him, "it would be a betrayal of her love." (LTL, 120).

In early September, Merton makes what he calls "a sort of retreat" before his permanent commitment as a hermit. He decides to go over these journal entries to see whether he can "make any sense out of it or see my affair in any kind of perspective." As a result of doing so, he concludes: "God has been most good to us and has greatly protected us against ourselves—and has brought our love to a kind of quiet stability I think—so that we can go on more or less safely. And perhaps I don't need to fuss over it so much." (LTL, 125)

A phone call Merton made to Margie from the Cincinnati train station on September 10 was a "...happy, cheerful, friendly, affectionate call without hooks and without anguish, and without smoke." (LTL, 131)

While the call left Merton somewhat guilty (because it was surreptitious), he also considered it right and just to Margie: "It was 'owed'" (LTL, 133)

Letters from Margie and another from Sister K, (probably someone from the hospital), though marked as "conscience matter," had been opened by monastery personnel. The letter from Sister K concerning how Margie had received his communication was something of a consolation to him: "You are saving, in your love and suffering, the one you love." (LTL, 134)

In October, he received a letter from Margie that was "Sweet and warm and loving—with a complete and total love." It touched him, and yet it seemed to underline the fact that he was a solitary, a hermit; he cannot explain "...how I can love her and be a hermit...." (LTL, 145)

Again when they met that October (when Margie was in Kentucky to take exams), he became aware that the short time they had together then was all they could ever hope to have from now on. He realized: "For the first time since April, I can see that the affair is no longer so intense, and I feel much freer. Yet I hate it to stop...." (LTL, 151)

A few days later he realizes that "...it is clearly *over*. Except for friendship, I hope, and the last communication that may be required to avoid bitterness and bad feeling about it." (LTL, 154)

In November, he writes about a letter from Margie that communicates for him the reality of her love and of their love for one another. As he stands weeping in the early snowfall, he reminds himself of their mutual significance and value: "I have to admit our love as a basic and central truth about which there can be no nonsense." He goes on to say that he must face three realities: a passion that might become disruptive, the fact of his vocation to a deep mystical life, and the fact of Margie's genuine love. He adds: "God alone can reconcile all that has to be reconciled." (LTL, 157)

On December 20, Merton writes about a call to Margie he felt had been right to make. The outcome of it was curious to him. He seemed to be aware of and willing to critique a quality in her that he had not previously noted. He names this quality a discrepancy between the simple inmost self he loves and her "superimposed, determined, aggressive little persona." He summarizes their exchange as an evolution in their relating to one another and comments that "in our minds we still grasp on ideas of each other as we want ourselves to have been when it was best." (LTL, (172-173)

We do not hear the romantic lover in Merton any longer here:

This is not for me. I have my way to follow. If it becomes a choice…I am not sure whether it has to, but anyway, this suggestion [from Margie to resist the Abbot] gets nothing from me but "No." I have my vocation to follow, and it is on a level she does not really take into account…. Can she take it seriously? (LTL, 173)

But then he goes on to remind himself of "the reality of that inner M that I can never, never repudiate." And he adds realistically: "Her body is young and hungers. Mine is middle-aged and has its wild moments and its desperations too. There is the danger. The real danger. And now I know it." (LTL, 173)

Reading his journal, we are clearly aware that their relationship is cooling off and winding down. His growing perspective on the past few months testifies to that. During the Christmas holidays he is lonely for Margie, but he resists calling her, saying to himself, "No end to it. But if we don't get impatient, things will quietly work out with no fracas—and with a deep and lasting union of hearts." (LTL, 175)

On December 30, Merton calls Margie again, away from the monastery as was becoming his practice in contacting her. While in Louisville later the same day he calls her a second time because he was missing her and listening to a juke box record called "Together Again." He wrote that it would be a struggle "to get all this straight." (LTL, 177)

Margie tells him she may move to Hawaii for a year, which he assumes will provide an obvious end to their regular contact. On New Year's Day, as he turns a leaf of his journal to 1967, he writes that it is a bit optimistic to claim that their relationship is free of complication and adds, "I am lucky that it is not much more complex than it is." (LTL, 182)

On February 4, Merton went into town, to the doctor where

he hoped to get in touch with Margie but couldn't. This made him decide "it is time to stop fooling, finally, with letters and phone calls." (LTL, 191)

But again, he fails to take the advice he has given himself. He calls Margie on March 7 and is disappointed with himself for stating to her the obvious: that they have moved into a new phase in their relationship. On Holy Thursday, March 23, he lies in bed remembering a call to her a week previously from Lexington, one without passion and no longer troubling to him. On March 30, he phones her and reports only factually that Margie is moving into an apartment with a friend.

On April 21, Merton again calls Margie from a place called the Brown Hotel and hears that her fiancé is back in the picture, and she tells him that she is planning to marry him. Merton is disturbed when she tells him she does not exactly love this man but feels she can make him happy. She accuses herself of being a sort of masochist. Merton decides to keep out of it, which he calls taking their fading relationship "another inexorable step." (LTL, 222)

He notes that the only feeling left now in him is a real loneliness, something he must accept. He writes in the journal on Pentecost Sunday that the "sin" he sees in himself is "...*unawareness*, lostness, slackness, relaxation, dissipation of desire, lack of courage and decision." (LTL, 236)

We wonder, considering Merton's many entries about the validity of monastic life in general, whether this "sin" is only around his relationship with Margie. Does it, perhaps, now extend to his avoidance of a decision on whether or not he should remain in religious life at all? Should his assessment of the sickness he sees in the Gethsemani community be telling him to leave? Is his angst no longer about Margie, but about an authentic call to leave the monastery? There seems no answer to those questions.

On May 17, Merton phones Margie again, though he is uncertain about the wisdom of doing so "with much affection or so frequently." (LTL, 237)

He comments on the fact that things are calming down and that she sounded happy. On June 10, they talk about meeting in Louisville a couple of weeks later, but he thinks they are both reluctant to do so, and he wants to get out of it.

On June 21, he calls her from the University of Louisville and finds she is no longer planning to marry her fiancé. She encourages him to leave in order to be himself, and her words lead him to consider that possibility.

Finally, however, he writes that "...there is really nowhere else I want to live but in this hermitage." (LTL, 253-254)

He goes on to comment that the year before, when he was seeing Margie regularly, was one of the best as far as his health was concerned. Now his "revolt against my predicament here" (LTL, 254) no longer has her presence to ease those physical issues.

On June 25 he writes: "I definitely do not intend to try to see M. or do anything more about her—maybe call once in a while to see how she is doing, that's all." (LTL, 255)

The very last entry relating to Merton's contact with Margie was on August 1, 1967, after translating for one of the monastery visitors:

> He talked about how easily we forget those we love on earth, and as I walked up through the field I was thinking of M, as if that were the kind of love he meant. I haven't been in contact with her for over a month—and have no plans for getting in contact in the near future. Yet I wondered how she is. (LTL, 270-271)

Clearly from these entries, we see that Merton had not only decided but also had acted upon his decision to end the relationship with Margie in his own way and on his own terms. There seems to be something natural about the gradual waning of the intensity they had experienced, and many who have experienced a similar need to move on in their lives might well agree that this was the kinder, more humane way to act. We can never know, of course, if that assessment was accurate; we can only know it was the one Merton chose.

XVII

Merton might have written:

I said when this began
That it was dangerous,
And it was.
I could have lost everything:
The one place on earth
Where I belong,
That home, the one
That's like a nest
Of all that's right
Inside me,
Where I, really, can go.
Yet just look what I did
To her:
A flood of promises from
My words, my actions,
My body
That I could never keep.
Funny,
Nuts though it was
I can't say I have regrets;
I'm not sure why,
And that's the strangest thing of all,
The most mysterious.

Merton did write:

February 22, 1967

Certainly a great deal has changed. In many ways we have swung around 180 degrees from the attitude that prevailed when I entered. Good or bad? Both. Neither. The old ways had to be changed but I do not know if the new makes sense. I find that I certainly do not believe in the monastic life as I did when I entered—and when I was more sure I knew what it was. Yet I am much more convinced I am doing more or less what I ought to do, though I don't know why and cannot fully justify it." (LTL, 201)

. . . .

I now write:

Far from being just a love story about a middle-age man and a twenty-something woman, Merton's journal tells of the maturing of a monastic vocation. Woven throughout the daily entries, and prominent in *Midsummer Diary for M*, we read of the dissatisfaction and disillusionment Merton was experiencing at Gethsemani. That is, perhaps, the main reason he was ready to meet a real woman, to find and express mutual love for another human being, to know the joy and anguish and imperfection of his complete incarnation as a spirit enfleshed. Moreover, he was also a man at that point in his life where the limitation of human institutions, no matter the good intentions of their members, could possibly satisfy him.

Sam Keen uses the word "outlaw" to describe someone who

has reached the point Keen calls "the phase beyond adulthood." The outlaw moves outside and beyond any institutions in which he or she functions, at least somewhat comfortably, to enter into a new period of development. This metaphor reminds me of Merton's certainty that it was right to open himself to this relationship with Margie, despite its apparent contradiction with his vowed life. Margie led him to risk setting aside what Keen calls "the mores of the tribe." (Keen, 130)

Merton's old life, which had been embraced so willingly for so long, now seemed to him, as Keen would say, empty, boring, and meaningless. A person at this point in life will often turn to romance of some kind as a way to avoid experiencing these feelings.

This is not to deny the realization Merton had come to: that he had never felt the need for, nor allowed himself to be vulnerable with, a woman. Such an admission of his inability to love or feel loved was for him a realization of his deficiency as a human and spiritual being, a block to embracing the depths of his good and true self. It highlights the significance of the choice he made to risk Margie's love for him and his for her. The "wrongness" and, at the same time, the "rightness" of this decision were the two things he never was able to deny throughout the pages of his journal.

On another level, that of Merton's journey to spiritual wholeness, we might wonder whether Margie's entry at this point in his life was something of an affirmation about his increasing disillusionment with the monastery he had once so enthusiastically embraced. The need for feminine influence he expressed shortly before Margie came on the scene perhaps set the stage for an invitation to avoid, at least for a time, just how much the life of solitary living beyond monastic community demands. Perhaps that is why he had to admit—though he couldn't articulate why—she was inexorably part of his hermit vocation. Early on, Merton saw that their relationship could never be enough for him, never fill the need for solitude which had been so long his desire. This realization may have been what encouraged him to walk even further into the darkness and mystery of his hermit vocation. And, ironically, Margie who could not fulfill that need in him turned out to provide him with the strength and love he required to follow his true path. Without the experience of his lovableness and his worth, could he have stood so alone before God, confident in Divine mercy? Merton seems to have both needed Margie for a time and then needed to let her go. Michael Mott in his official biography of Merton says it succinctly: "the story has a moral beyond morals. 'The love of creatures' (to use a phrase from Merton's old style) is seldom wise. Sometimes we learn great wisdom in loving unwisely." (Mott, 438)

Merton seems to have decided to leave the entire affair at that. So must we, unless we think we know him better than he knew himself, this man of profound contemplative awareness who was willing to share his most intimate thoughts with us. Margie, at least in Merton's view expressed at the time of his *Midsummer Diary for M*, seems willing to accept what he sees as her agreement to his assessment: "She asks of my solitude that it have in it a place for her in which she is always known, reverenced, loved, valued, prized for herself as she is in her actuality. I will never refuse her this...." (LTL, 311)

Margie was never a feminine distraction for Merton; she was a real woman whom he promised never to forget, whatever their future turns out to be. We have absolutely no reason to believe he did not fulfill that vow. Late in his *Midsummer Diary for M.* he affirms her enduring presence when he says "She will be my love but in this absurd and special way: as part of the 'realization' which is solitude." (LTL, 322)

If this last statement was mysterious to Merton, how much more so must it have been to Margie. He goes on to remark about his overly-analytical self: "Life is not futile if you simply live it. It remains futile, however, as long as you keep watching yourself live it." One can only wonder what she made of these statements of his, insightful though they surely were for him, at least in moments of clarity. He wants her to know how significant she has been and always will be: "I cannot regard this as 'just an episode.' It is a profound event in my life and one which will have entered deeply into my heart to alter and transform my whole climate of thought and experience: for in her I realize I had found something, someone, that I had been looking for all my life." (LTL, 328)

Merton is surely writing here for himself, but he is also writing for Margie to read and be consoled by the words, even as he has to add in honesty, "I am supposed to be lonely and live alone, and sleep alone, so I have no problem and no complaint. It is merely what I have chosen and the choice is ratified over and over each day." (LTL, 329)

Merton's message to Margie is one of enduring love but not of possession. Frequently he returns to the reminder that he does not expect her to live alone, nor does he want her to be lonely. Hers is a different path from his, at least at that time in her life and with her different vocation. He tells her, "I know you will always have a special love for me, but though you have told me not to say this, I will say it anyway because I have to: I cannot possibly consider you committed in any way solely to me. That would really be an injustice and an absurdity." (LTL, 346)

The framework and boundaries of their relationship were set by June of 1966, the time when he gave her the *Midsummer Diary for M.* This document was something written as much for him as for her, even in its style of personal reflection along with direct address to her. What he said in it was very clear, and he wanted Margie to know exactly where he stood. Whether he himself took it to heart seems doubtful, as manifested by his future actions. The behavior that followed for both of them in the next several seemed to hope for and ask for something different.

XVIII

Some things
You never face
Until you're alone,
And only then when
All avenues of escape are closed.
The radical Self,
The one who saves you
And all the others
And is Christ
And who you are
Hides under the stories
You tell yourself with their
Half lies.
It's hard to distinguish
Vibrant, breathing aloneness
From dead loneliness.
At least hard for me.
Am I abandoned to my
False self?
Or to my
True one?
This question hermits face
And probably never answer
For sure.
At least I don't.
Alone or lonely;
I can't be sure.
Perhaps both.

Merton did write:

Letter to Friends, 1967

I have made commitments which are unconditional and cannot be taken back. I do not regard this position as especially courageous: it is just the ordinary stuff of life, the acceptance of limits which we must all accept in one way or another: the acceptance of a sphere in which one is called to love, trust, and believe and pray—and meet those whom one is destined to meet and love." (Merton, A Life in Letters, 321)

. . . .

I now write:

The virtue of humility, so foundational for the monastic person, might be described in various ways, one of which is "groundedness in truth." Ordinary reality is often a disappointment to people who prefer to experience life on the event horizon of emotion and energy. For them, even anguish can sometimes appear more palatable than the mundane. When the romance of life fades, as it did for Merton before his encounter with Margie, the contemplative is faced with personal as well as situational limitations—seeing what one is: a creature. While spiritual masters may possess many gifts, as Thomas Merton surely did, he or she is still faced with the boundaries that humanity, by definition, imposes.

When life loses its entertaining possibilities, the good thing that is meant to result for the contemplative is a quiet contentment with the real. Perhaps one symbol of this honest appraisal of one's self for a monastic person is the daily repetitive Liturgy of the Hours, whether said in choir or even alone (as it often turned out to be for Merton in his hermit life). The quiet depths beneath the words of that ancient prayer make silence the only possible, although mostly inarticulate, response. The contemplative knows that what happens in prayer to transform any person who lives a humble, simple, ordinary existence cannot be adequately expressed, only experienced.

Merton had lived the contemplative life for many years before he met Margie. At this period in his life, however, he felt called to move beyond life in community to a more solitary form of monasticism, that of the hermit. Reflecting on this second call, one he had followed and sealed as a commitment the previous year, he writes early in 1967:

> Maybe the hermit life is another kind of defeat—but I certainly feel that here I am relatively more honest and more true than anywhere else and that here I am not being 'had'—and though I may be in many ways wrong, I am at least able honestly to try and cope with my wrongness here. (LTL, 199)

This reflection follows Merton's thoughts on why he had left the secular world and explained why he now feels he must leave even the fellowship of the monks. He is finding the monastery another form of sham, though not as bad as many others he has experienced, and he surely does not want to be any part of even a holy sham any longer. What he thought monastic life was when he entered Gethsemani and what he has come to see it is over time are worlds apart from one another. He no longer can even define for himself its purpose.

St. Benedict in his Rule provides a way for certain monastics to move beyond the community aspect of the monastery to embrace a solitary hermit existence. Merton drew on that exception when he proposed his own choice, and he was able, after some difficulty, to obtain permission for his hermitage. The hermit life for St. Benedict was allowed when a monk has "lived through the test of living in a monastery for a long time, and [has] passed beyond the first fervor of monastic life." (Rule of St. Benedict, 169)

The description of such a monk (articulated in fifth century vocabulary) continues: "Self-reliant now, without the support of another, they are ready with God's help to grapple single-handed with the vices of body and mind." (Rule of St. Benedict, 169)

Merton called the life of the hermit a kind of absurdity and himself absurd to embrace it. In his *Midsummer Diary for M*, he says to her, and maybe even more so to himself: "What does the lonely and absurd man have to teach others? Simply that being alone and absurd are not things to be feared." He has come to realize that "Everybody remains secretly absurd and alone. Only no one dares face the fact. Yet facing this fact is the absolutely essential requirement for beginning to live freely." (LTL, 322)

We wonder now what new depths of this awareness of his hermit vocation Merton had found and was writing about since Margie had come on the scene; even she had clearly been not enough to make him forget his "absurdity." In fact, ultimately, she only underlined it. In May of 1967 he wrote:

The deep inner sustaining power of silence. When I taste this again, so surely, after so long, I know what it means to repent of my infidelity and foolishness: yet at the same time I do not try to build up again anything that was properly torn down. It was good that I (we) went through the storm: it was the only way to learn a truth that was otherwise inaccessible. (LTL, 217-218)

In September of 1967, he wrote: "So I choose to continue in the hermitage under conditions that are from a certain viewpoint political, fraudulent (i.e. on the part of authority)." This last parentheses refers to the "inner, deep problem" of staying as part of Gethsemani under Dom James administration. (LTL, 285)

But in the end it all seems to boil down to the reality for Merton that he likes his life and sees no real reason—not even his love for Margie—to look for anything else, no reason to cut off all ties to his monastery. His monastic vow of stability experienced in his sense of "at homeness" where he is, echoes through this passage of May, 1967:

> *Peace, silence, freedom of heart, no care, quiet joy. Last year—there was joy and turbulence and trouble which turned to confusion and a deeply disturbed heart because I knew I was wrong and was going against everything I lived for. Today I looked up at the tall treetops and the high clouds and listened to the silence—and was very glad indeed to be alone! What idiocy I got into last year. (LTL, 227)*

But Margie remains part of his life in his place as he adds, "Still I wonder how she is, and what is developing in her life. I worry a little about her." (LTL, 227)

And so it ends. The story of one of the world's great mystics and his very human love for a woman he could never truly have. Thank you, Thomas, and you too, Margie, for sharing it with us.

EPILOGUE

Thomas Merton did write:

Letter to Friends, 1967

In actual fact I have never seriously considered leaving the church and though the question of leaving the monastic state has presented itself, I was not able to take it seriously for more than five or ten minutes. (Merton, A Life in Letters, 321)

. . . .

I now write:

Thomas Merton burned his letters from Margie without even re-reading them before he set out for Asia in 1968. (Mott, 533) Perhaps they held no longer any significance for him, although that seems impossible to imagine. Perhaps he did so to insure that, for her, there would remain anonymity breached only if she would choose to do so. For himself, however, he clearly intended revealing this important aspect of his life twenty-five years after his death. Along with his other journals, this one stands as a revelation of the honesty he sought for himself and those who would read his words. I have found that Christine Bochen in her introduction to *Learning to Love*, provides the best summary of its entries:

This journal shows him as he was: capable of profundity and pettiness, sensitivity and self-absorption, insight and illusion, focus and distraction. What sets him apart is the expansiveness of his spirit and his candor. Perhaps by telling his story, he invites us to reflect on our own stories. In learning to love, Merton was made to explore the very depths of solitude and freedom, and, perhaps, by sharing his exploration with us, he invites us to do the same. (LTL, xxiii)

There remains only for me to share what I have discovered in writing this volume. Through the repeated back and forth of Merton's thinking it might at first seem that he held out for a long period of time the possibility of an enduring relationship with Margie. In fact, not only in the "Letter to Friends," which I have quoted above, but also in his repeated and clearly articulated awareness in his journal, we see that this was not the case. Marriage was quickly out of the question and, though toyed with for a somewhat longer period, he was never going to leave the monastery, as he admitted fairly early on. What followed this acknowledgment was the hope—or maybe better put, an optimistic fantasy—that he and Margie could spend their lives in some sort of a compromise loving relationship. Merton's genuine care soon gave way to the realization that to plan for such an outcome would keep Margie kept enslaved to a vocation that was his, but not hers.

I would also say that this part of Merton's journal might have looked to some, and even perhaps to me in my earlier, more cursory readings, primarily the tale of a romance. It has, however, turned out for me to be much more than that. It is evident that it is the story of a vocation, one that was questioned and, in the questioning, deepened. I should have anticipated as much from a man like Thomas Merton. The picture he leaves us here is of a re-commitment to a calling received many years earlier and with no knowledge of what that dedication would one day demand. Many people, of course, can identify with such an experience: original promises made to someone—perhaps another human being and perhaps God—have a significance and power beyond even their generous intent.

While it was impossible for Merton to put into adequate words why he chose to remain monastic, he kept trying to do so. I believe he succeeded more than he thought he had. What at first looked, to me at least, like stark resignation to remain true to his vows, gradually gave way to the conviction of his simple and peaceful joy and contentment in the choice he had made. As a Zen master would say, "This is it." It doesn't really matter what words Merton chose to describe his final choice; it is clear he finally relaxed more deeply than ever before into silence and contemplation before he died.

I do wonder how Merton's life would have played out if he had lived more than two more years after this experience with Margie. Would his relationship with her have opened him to a new relationship with some other woman, perhaps one grounded in a commitment to life as a religious? Would such mutual commitment have shown them ways to balance their vowed dedication with deep intimacy? Or would he have retreated even more into his solitude, fearing to ever again become vulnerable with another? This we will never know, of course. Nor is it important that we do.

Perhaps these words, among the torrent he wrote, might be helpful: "I must manfully face this judgment [of right or wrong] and find my center not in an ideal self which just *is* (fully realized), but in an actual self which does all it can to be honest and to love truly, though it still may fail." (LTL, 78)

The search for the true self, wherever that may take a person, is a solitary one. It is never finished, because it always involves new considerations as life unfolds. Merton was willing to share his own experience, his self-deceptions and his honest admissions, and his discernments around his false self and his true self. He found the answer that he decided was right for him. That seems to be all that he intended to do. At least it is all anyone can realistically expect from these pages: a picture of a man who acknowledged and risked imperfection in a commitment to becoming human.

As for Margie, it is so ironic that she—not the monk—is the one who has practiced silence in all this! I want to thank her for loving Thomas Merton and teaching him that he was lovable and capable of loving her. I hope that she, too, found her own truth.

RESOURCES

Baudoz, Jean-Francois, *With Christ* (Collegeville, MN: Liturgical Press, 2005).

Benedict, Saint, *RB 80, The Rule of St. Benedict* (Collegeville, MN: Liturgical Press, 1981).

Keen, Sam, *The Passionate Life: Stages of Loving* (New York: Harper and Row, 1983).

Merton, Thomas, *Eighteen Poems* (New York: New Directions, 1968).

Merton, Thomas, *Learning to Love, Vol. 6, 1966-1967*, ed. Christine Bochen. (New York: HarperCollins, 1997). Includes *Midsummer Diary for M.* References in this book: LTL

Merton, Thomas, *Love and Living* (New York: Farrar, Straus, Giroux, 1979). References in this book: LAL

Merton, Thomas, *The Seven Storey Mountain* (New York: Harcourt Brace, 1948).

Mott, Michael, *The Seven Mountains of Thomas Merton* (Boston: Houghton Mifflin, 1984).

Rohr, Richard, *Immortal Diamond* (San Francisco: Jossey-Bass, 2013).

Zuercher, Suzanne, *Merton, An Enneagram Profile* (Zuercher, 1996).

A NOTE FROM THE PUBLISHER

"God wants you to publish my book."

So said Sister Suzanne Zuercher the first time I met her about a year ago at a meeting of the Illinois Thomas Merton Society.

This is not the first time I have heard this opinion expressed. I am a publisher and I do publish books on spirituality. And a lot of people believe that God wants or even tells them to write their books, so it is not surprising that they would also think that God would direct me to publish it.

Just for the record, this statement normally does not convince me to publish a book. In fact it usually has the opposite effect. I figure if God wanted me to publish a particular book, he also would have notified me. At least a heads up by email or text! But this has never happened to me.

But this time, for some reason, it was different.

Sr. Suzanne was a pretty persuasive lady. When I met her she was 82 years old, a Benedictine nun all her adult life, the former head of a high school, a psychologist, life coach, and spiritual director, and the noted writer of several books. She was also an expert on the Enneagram and on Thomas Merton's writing. Plus she has a great sense of humor, even about her belief that God wanted me to publish her book, although she claimed she truly believed that.

After reading her manuscript, I agreed to produce her book under our brand new In Extenso imprint. But it turned out that Sr. Suzanne was then in a big hurry to get it printed. Merton's 100th birthday was coming up in January of 2015, she pointed out, and she wanted the book out well before then. I'm not sure she told me God demanded it be published so quickly, but Sr. Suzanne certainly did. As I have mentioned, she is very persuasive. So I put her book at the front of our editorial pipeline and began working on it.

While her book was in the final stages of typesetting, Sr. Suzanne was unexpectedly diagnosed with serious cancer. I was able to get the book printed and copies sent to her before she went in for her operation. I am told seeing the book gave her great pleasure. She never really recovered, however, and died peacefully on June 14, 2014.

May her soul, and the souls of all the faithful departed, through the Mercy of God, rest in peace. Amen.

Gregory F. Augustine Pierce
Publisher, ACTA Publications

OTHER BOOKS FOR
THE CONTEMPLATIVE-IN-THE-WORLD

THE ART OF PAUSING
Meditations for the Overworked and Overwhelmed
Judith Valente, Brother Paul Quenon, OCSO, and Michael Bever

Haiku poems on the 99 Names of God found in various faith traditions accompanied by a reflection or an abstract photo. Paperback, $14.95.

GRACE REVISITED
Epiphanies from a Trappist Monk
James Stephen Behrens, OCSO

Stories of people, places, and events that have touched the life of a Trappist monk at the Monastery of the Holy Spirit in Conyers, Georgia. Paperback, $14.95

RUNNING INTO THE ARMS OF GOD
THE GEOGRAPHY OF GOD'S MERCY
THE LONG YEARNING'S END
Patrick Hannon, CSC

This trilogy of stories of the presence of God in daily life looks at love-in-action. Three separate paperbacks, $12.95 each

STORIES
John Shea

All of the stories written and told by theologian and storyteller John Shea, now in a single volume. Paperback, $14.95.

THE MESSAGE
Catholic/Ecumenical Edition
Eugene Peterson, with William Griffin

A fresh, compelling, insightful, challenging, faith-filled paraphrasal translation of the complete Bible (including the deuterocanonical books), directly from the ancient languages into modern, idiomatic English. Paperback, $29.95; hardcover, $37.95